HE WAS MY BROTHER

PETER DICKSON

Peter Dickson

He Was My Brother

ISBN: 978-1-922890-68-9

For Ness, Abby, Sasha and Luke

Contents

Prologue		1
Chapter 1	Sickly	5
Chapter 2	Happy Days	14
Chapter 3	The NSCA	22
Chapter 4	The Missionary	28
Chapter 5	The Hawks	33
Chapter 6	The Perfect Storm	40
Chapter 7	The Turps	45
Chapter 8	Your Move	52
Chapter 9	One in Eight Million	57
Chapter 10	Hush Productions	64
Chapter 11	The Passion To Play	74
Chapter 12	Survivor	83
Chapter 13	Celebrity	94
Chapter 14	AFL Hall of Fame	101
Chapter 15	Access All Areas	106
Chapter 16	The Collapse	110
Chapter 17	Rob Dickson Productions	114
Chapter 18	Essence of the Game	119

Chapter 19	The Call	131
Chapter 20	South Africa	137
Chapter 21	The Memorial	145
Chapter 22	AFL Season Launch	153
Chapter 23	AFL House	159
Chapter 24	Fifty of You	170
Chapter 25	What Now?	176
Chapter 26	Forged in Fire	181
Chapter 27	On the Couch	197
Chapter 28	Two Nations, One Obsession	205
Chapter 29	Spud	210
Chapter 30	The Ripple Effect	217
Chapter 31	The Profession	221
Chapter 32	Filmmaker Or Dud?	224
Epilogue		230

Foreword

Pete Dickson is an incredibly talented filmmaker. I have known him now for two decades and my admiration for his work and his immense artistic contribution to our country only continue to grow.

More importantly, Pete is a wonderful person. He is a loving father, husband, son and brother who is part of a big family. All families can speak of the love and the pain that you witness across the years, how you deal with the challenges of life and the difficulties of coping with tragedy, and the long-term impact that events can have upon you.

In this book, Pete honours the life of his late brother Rob, his hero and his best friend. It tells exquisitely the story of his own journey through life, from the child finding his own way in a big family, to an adult finding his way in a big world.

At times it's tough, and at other times it's joyous. It is filled with triumph, disappointment, happiness and terrible grief, and is a compelling story I urge you to read because it centres around love.

Gillon McLachlan. CEO, Australian Football League.

PROLOGUE

My body is trembling uncontrollably. I've abruptly awoken, my eyes are trying to focus but it's pitch black and every inch of me is violently shaking. This is something I've never experienced. I feel I must be having a heart attack, not that I know what it feels like to have a heart attack, but it was my best guess. Sheer panic engulfs me, and I am hyperventilating. What is going on? Am I dying?

I struggle out of bed and fall to my knees as I attempt to stand. My heartbeat is rapid. Far too rapid I decide. I try to call out to my wife, Ness, for help. But nothing comes out of my mouth, it's an almighty effort even to take a breath, let alone speak. Yelling out would be pointless anyway as Ness is sleeping in another room because of being on call overnight in her job as an obstetrician. Even with my best efforts she would never hear me.

I have to get to her. I somehow manage to drag myself down the hallway and crash into the room where Ness is in a deep

1

sleep. It's a rude awakening. Scarcely awake, she tries to gather herself and establish what the hell is happening. Ness has never seen me so frightened and pulls me on to the bed, holding me tight until the shaking starts slowly to subside. I am in the midst of a nervous breakdown.

Only a few hours later I am being examined by my GP who prescribes Valium and other medications to immediately try to calm my system. The following day I find myself on a psychiatrist's couch for the first time in my life. The words of my soon to be regular psychiatrist, Dr Chris Walsh, prove a chilling wake-up call, 'If you don't get help immediately, you will be dead within twelve months.'

7 AM, THURSDAY 30 NOVEMBER 2017.

I tap nervously on the steering wheel as I drive into the city from my home in Hawthorn. Anxious because I am on my way to the RSN Radio studio for an interview on Daniel Harford's breakfast show. We are promoting my coming documentary release on Channel Nine called *Forged in Fire*, a three-part series on the history of the Ashes I had made for Cricket Australia.

Part of the job of making documentaries is to spruik them once completed. I had conducted many of these before but it's still an element of the process with which I've never been overly comfortable. This was my fourteenth sports documentary broadcast release since my brother and filmmaking partner, Rob, and his two sons tragically died in a car accident, eight years earlier in 2009. He was on my mind as I weaved my way through traffic. I was thinking how he used to love this part, as he was very comfortable with himself on radio or television. I guess it came with the territory after many years of life as an AFL player, a sports filmmaker, and a reality TV show winner on *Australian Survivor*.

Though uneasy, I am looking forward to catching up and speaking with Daniel Harford, an old friend of Robs and host of the breakfast show. Listening to the station on the way in I hear my name mentioned as coming on air soon. I smiled, thinking many of those listening would be asking 'Who?' Rob Dickson was well known, Peter Dickson not so much. Documentary makers are not exactly household names. I was mentally still very fragile from the breakdown episode a few months earlier. Treatment and medication were helping immensely, but I still had a long road to travel with the demons and suppressed grief lurking within.

After a typical warm welcome from Daniel, I'm soon on air discussing all things *Forged in Fire*. As we were chatting, one of Daniel's co-hosts started to talk about the process of making these documentaries. I vividly remember a point within the interview where he looked at me and said 'so everyone considers you a filmmaker' in what felt to me like a manner or tone that suggested he didn't. At that stage, because of what I was going through, I had maximum levels of sensitivity to any negativity. In hindsight I was probably imagining it but at the time I sensed a strong insinuation that he wasn't convinced.

He continued with, 'But what is it that you actually do? So

you're the one who's sitting down and asking all the questions?' I'm thinking this bloke doesn't rate me, this is getting awkward. I responded with, 'Yes, I do all the interviews for my films, I write, produce and direct and then edit.' (The only element of making a documentary I rarely, if ever, take on is physically holding the camera, there are far more skilled camera operators than me that's for certain). With that he seemed genuinely surprised and somewhat satisfied that maybe I was a filmmaker, but I cannot be sure.

As I was leaving the studio, Daniel gave me a warm bear hug goodbye, his love of Rob still patently evident. But from the moment I stepped into the elevator I couldn't get that line of questioning out of my mind. Was I really a filmmaker or merely a try-hard? Was I any good at what I do or was I a dud? Why was I continuing this manic quest of trying to reach Rob's level of storytelling and quality in what I made?

It was ridiculous. I knew I had an audience who enjoyed my docos, even winning awards for them, so there shouldn't be a lot more to try to prove. But I was still triggered. The insecurities and overwhelming self-doubt of following in my dead brother's footsteps, trying to keep his filmmaking legacy alive, took hold of me again. This lifelong chase to be his equal hadn't ended.

CHAPTER 1

SICKLY

He stood poised at the microphone knowing full well he had the room in the palm of his hands. Clearing his throat, he shot me a glance which I knew all too well. It was coming, he was winding up and about to mock and ridicule me in the nicest possible way. His ability to deride, without offending, was elite.

It was May 2002 and Rob was seconds away from delivering his best man speech at my wedding. As expected, he kicked off with a bang. 'Let's be honest…Pete has some issues.' The room erupted into hysterical laughter and I could see his face beaming, he was off and running thinking he was Jerry Seinfeld.

He then doubled down. 'My first memories of Pete, who is five years younger than me, was that he was a very sickly child.' This time it took about five minutes for the crowd to calm down and stop laughing. Rob was in no rush to move on and was clearly basking in the pandemonium echoing around the function room. I was seated at the main table, doing my best to act as though I wasn't fussed at all. Problem was my bright red face and awkward smile belied the persona I was trying to roll with. But he was accurate. I was a very sickly child.

Thirty-four years earlier in the Box Hill Hospital, Melbourne, Effie Dickson was in the final stages of labour about to give birth to her fifth child, me. Right next to her in the same room in another bed was her sister Elizabeth, who only ten hours earlier had birthed my cousin Warwick. What are the odds? Two sisters giving birth within ten hours of each other in the same room. Effie had endured a difficult and painful fortnight of falling in and out of labour, so was filled with relief when this chubby fair skinned new addition to the Dickson clan finally entered the arena.

I am one of six children to Effie and Rick Dickson. There was one girl (Sue) and five boys (Graham, Don, Rob, me, and younger brother Ricky). Poor Sue. I mean, really? One girl and five boys seems ridiculously unlucky to me. Mum and dad always wanted a big family, well maybe mum more so than dad. Myth has it that dad told mum she could decide the name of any girls and he would look after the name of any boys. Mum was off to a flyer with Sue, but then boy after boy was born. Mum had to put her foot down in the naming stakes by the time I arrived and declared the deal no longer fair, and so she named me Peter. She always told me it meant the rock. Growing up it made me proud to think I was solid like a rock, it resonated with me, I liked the feeling of that.

In those early years we lived in Heathmont, an outer suburb

of Melbourne. My father was a finance executive and mum was at home taking care of six kids. Dad was also a sportsman of note across baseball and cricket. He was first selected to national honours for Australia in baseball back in 1960. Sport was in the genes. His father, Norm, had played VFL with Richmond in the 1930s, rucking alongside the great Jack Dyer. Mum was a beautiful looking woman, very athletic in her own right with strong Christian beliefs. Football was also in her family genes, her brother Duncan Wright having played VFL footy as a tough and talented Collingwood back flanker.

My early memories of childhood in Heathmont include being outside all day every day, trying to keep up with my siblings in whatever they were doing. Sport played a massive role in our youth, we all seemed to inherit those sporting genes so it was a very competitive household. We were constantly on skateboards, bikes, kicking the footy, playing cricket, watching Graham attempt the most outrageously dangerous stunts, and spending hours on end in our three-storey treehouse in the backyard.

We had a game called 'kick the tin' which often had every kid on the block join in. It was a hide and seek game on steroids. Kids would be hiding in any house of their choosing. Everyone knew everyone in the neighbourhood, and we always felt very safe out and about. I can still hear the noise of lawn mowers in the distance on a Saturday morning. I still love that sound. If I smell freshly cut grass today it takes me back in time. Memories of rushing outside with unbridled excitement when we heard the chimes of a Mr Whippy Ice-Cream van are still crystal clear. It was always joyous if mum gave us fifty cents for a double cone instead of twenty-five cents for a single. When it came to dinner time mum would stand on the front steps of our small weatherboard home and scream 'Susan, Graham, Donald, Robert, Peter, Ricky – DINNER TIME!' Her voice heavenly like she was singing a hymn. You could hear her even if three streets away.

I remember thinking how lucky I was to be part of such a large family, and my older siblings were my heroes, especially Rob. From as early as I can remember we were always close; our personalities and humour were very similar. I would follow him around like a little puppy, trying to walk in his footsteps, the fact that I was constantly supplied his hand-me-down footwear meant I was literally walking in his footsteps. He was an extrovert of the highest order, I on the other hand sit firmly on the fence between introvert and extrovert. I can go either way, but he always had the ability to draw the extrovert out of me.

One particularly strong memory for me as a young boy was sunburn. Sunscreen application during the summer in the 1970s was something I cannot remember at any stage. Surrounded by siblings who had far more olive skin, meant that I sort of snuck under the radar and paid for it dearly. Mum dabbing milk on to my scorched body on a summer evening was commonplace. I'm still not sure what milk did for the skin but in her mind, it healed everything. She would then turn the old Westinghouse fan on to full throttle in the bedroom I shared with Rob and Ricky, bunk style. Something about that fan was very soothing and is still vivid in my mind, just the sound and breeze. I still use a fan to help me sleep to this day.

Not only was I the unlucky one born with the most sunburn worthy skin… unbeknown to everyone at the time was I was also born with kidney reflux disease. This essentially means that whenever I tried to pee my bladder would only empty so much, and the rest would flow unchecked back into the kidneys. This caused kidney failure. I was a skinny toddler who looked like I had a bowling ball firmly planted in my stomach. It was actually an enlarged right kidney, and it was slowly deteriorating. My left kidney was also twisted and only forty-five per cent functional, so I was a ticking time bomb. At the time, no one thought anything was wrong with me as by all reports I was healthy, a good eater, very active and full of joy and laughter. Apparently, I would smile and laugh at everything, and Rob was the one who would get me going the most. The only thing which might have been a red flag to some was that I was a bed-wetter. Not just a standard bed-wetter, but chronic. Good enough to be an Olympic gold medallist if there was a bed-wetting category. It turned out I had good reason with bad kidneys. Not sure what excuse some of my other brothers had at the time.

To think back on mum having to get up every single night for so many years to change sheets and pyjamas just flabbergasts me, especially now I'm a parent. I'm not sure I would be up to that without tipping into insanity. Despite all this, I felt loved and cared for in my big family. I have some joyous memories of my early childhood, but equally recall some of the torment. There was a strong force field of protection around me from my older siblings. It was needed. Our parents had a volatile relationship. In our house it was often like a tinder box ready to take flame and when it did it was frightening for young kids to witness. When the fighting inevitably erupted, Sue and the older boys would do their very best to try and shield us younger ones from what was going on. I know mum and dad loved us dearly.

I can't speak for my brothers and sister but from my perspective I always felt individually, they were loving and caring towards me. But it was a different story with each other. They truly tried to do the very best they could for us, but those traumatic experiences must have bred a reliance and trust within that my siblings would safeguard me. I have always felt protected by them. Always. As I grew older that never waned, especially from Rob. I feel eternally grateful and lucky to have had them surrounding me growing up.

After those early years in Heathmont, we moved as a family to Morwell, a small country town in Gippsland. Dad had been offered a senior position in Traralgon, not far from Morwell, as head of Esanda Finance. I was still in primary school, so the shift didn't affect me as much as my elder siblings. We arrived in Morwell and began life as country folk.

I remember Rob's first day in his new school, Morwell High. He came home black and blue, bruises all over his face and dried blood on his shirt. He was already a very good-looking rooster, very personable with a cheeky sense of humour. These traits didn't seem to go down too well with the locals at Morwell High School. Who was this upstart from the big smoke? Only one way to deal with him, with our fists.

For Rob, this was his first real taste of hate directed at him. He was a sensitive and compassionate soul from a young age, and the only punches he had received up until then were from his older brothers. This was different, it was venomous bullying and it bruised him in more ways than one. The outgoing and confident Rob disappeared. He was now in a place that was a world away from everything he knew before.

Mum and dad were mortified. It was only a matter of days before he and Don were taken out of Morwell High and enrolled into St Paul's College, Traralgon. At the time it was clearly the best school in the region. The problem for mum was that it was a strict Catholic school. As a fervent Methodist who took her children to church twice every Sunday (that was fun...), this was very hard for her to take. But she would do anything in her power to shield Rob from further suffering at Morwell High, even if it meant sending her kids to a Catholic school.

Meanwhile, I was settling into Morwell Primary School. This was where a few years later my kidney problem finally made its way to the surface. It was on a school camp in Grade 6 when I shared a room with three other boys. I was petrified of wetting the bed and embarrassing myself in front of the other lads. I knew I would. How could I not after visiting tinkle town every night for so many years? I remember holding on for dear life during the night at the school camp. The next morning with no sleep I was delighted I hadn't caused a little waterfall on to the lad sleeping in the bottom bunk.

It was only a few hours into the next morning when I started getting piercing pain through my stomach and back. The effort in holding on overnight had set something off inside. Mum and dad were away at the time and my grandparents were looking after the family at home. They were urgently called to pick me up from the camp as the teachers couldn't control the pain. Nan and Pa did their best to comfort me at home but I was deteriorating rapidly. Within a few days I was admitted to the Alfred Hospital in Melbourne for further testing. One week later I underwent major kidney surgery. A tube was successfully inserted between my bladder and kidney which ultimately fixed the reflux problem. That tube is still there to this day.

Most of my final year of primary school was spent in hospital followed by recuperation at home. From out of nowhere this was thrust upon the family and they all had to help this sickly kid get better. I remember a strong feeling of why me? All the other kids in my family are fine, why is it me who has copped this?

I don't remember too much from my time in hospital, but I do recall the day I was finally allowed to leave. Mum was eager to get me home but clearly nervous for the trip back to Morwell from Melbourne. I was still in serious pain, so any kind of movement ripped through me. This is a drive that should take about ninety minutes. Three hours later we were only halfway there. Travelling at an average speed of thirty kilometres an hour will do that. I still had bladder drainage bags attached and mum was petrified of hitting any bump and dislodging them. The sound of car horns and abuse from passing traffic can never be forgotten. Once back in Morwell and with my family again, it really hit home to me the severity of what had happened with my kidneys and how sickly I really was. Life for me would never be the same again.

Ricky and Rob had to subsequently undergo what was

a brutal kidney test back in the day, to see if they had any hereditary problems. Thankfully, they were given the all-clear, but never forgave me for having to undergo the dye tube inserted up the willy test. The operation was and has been a success and stopped the deterioration of my right kidney. I now had just enough function between my left and right kidney to stave off having to undertake dialysis, and I finally stopped wetting the bed.

CHAPTER 2

HAPPY DAYS

It was around this postoperative period that I started to become more emotionally connected and aware of life around me. Sue was now a schoolteacher, Graham a builder, Don had finished schooling and was a trainee golf professional. He would go on to become the first and only professional golfer in the Dickson clan. My little brother Ricky was strolling through primary school two years behind me, and Rob was appointed school captain of St-Paul's College in Year 10. The first non-Catholic ever to be named captain at St Paul's, which thrilled mum as a Methodist no end. She felt more than vindicated that switching schools for Rob was the best thing for him.

This school was a good fit for him. He had acquired a decent group of new mates and regained his spark during his secondary school years. This culminated in him being the top choice for school captain when the time came. It was a position and title Rob was incredibly proud of. For someone who hated to be disliked and wasn't afraid to be the centre of attention, this just built another layer on to the inner confidence he had always possessed.

In the meantime, I was trying to re-immerse myself into life while dealing with the constant fear that something might go wrong with my kidneys again. Before I had the operation, I was a sporting maniac, throwing myself into anything. My two particular loves were footy and cricket. Sport seemed to come very naturally which was simply luck and strong sporting genes. It was football where I was at my best. Rob was also developing into a good footballer, quick on his feet and very fond of leaping on shoulders.

I remember getting back into playing football as fast as I could once recuperated, but it felt different. I was very aware of my kidneys now. I played in the centre and felt like I could beat anyone. I was getting more and more confident as I progressed, not only in how I played the game but also in my kidneys. The worries I had were slowly drifting into the background. There were often local scouts watching games and I soon received a letter from AFL club Hawthorn inviting me to train with their junior squad (as we lived in the Hawthorn zone of the time). When dad handed over the envelope addressed to me with the Hawthorn Football Club insignia emblazoned across the top, my heart skipped a beat. For a young footy playing tragic that letter was gold, so much so that I still have it. The first Dickson boy to be asked to train with an AFL club. Even though it was just a request to train, it was the first step to me playing senior football for Hawthorn. There was no doubt in my naive youthful mind. I was convinced this was the path I was taking, even with this annoying kidney problem hanging heavily over me. It didn't go unnoticed by my brothers that I began to strut around like a peacock. My arms are still sore from the blows to pull my head in. I remember dad not being overly excited about the invitation and I wondered why.

The concern from the surgeons and medical experts treating me was contact to my kidney area. Any force could dislodge the tube and thus cause major ongoing problems. The threat of having to need kidney replacement surgery or live on a dialysis machine was real. The problem for me was each year I progressed it meant playing against bigger bodies. It came to a point where dad decided to put his foot down.

He made the call that I could play juniors up to the under-sixteens but no more footy after that. What? He surely could not be serious. I remember thinking he would change his mind, as this was ridiculous. But he didn't. He was adamant, no more football for me. I think back now and believe it was my very first bout of serious depression. It ripped me apart inside as I had significant ambitions with footy. I detested him, but also reluctantly understood the fears my family had. I think of what I would do now as a father myself if it were one of my children. I would do exactly what he did. He simply wanted his son to be safe and live a long healthy life. This became more evident to me as I grew older, and I respect him for that. In my final season I remember winning the best and fairest award, which upset me even more. I threw the trophy into the cupboard once home which snapped the little player statue off the top. It would be the last football trophy I ever won.

To see Rob drafted to Hawthorn a few years later and becoming an AFL player didn't help my state of mind. Even though thrilled and proud of him, there was definitely jealousy. What he achieved had been my childhood dream as well. I couldn't shake the feeling that I didn't even get a chance to at least try. The reality though is who can possibly know what would have happened. Like thousands of others who never made it to the elite level of sport, you think you could have, would have, should have. It's all moot, you didn't.

Years later when I had reached my early twenties, I was living with Rob who was still playing with Hawthorn. Football was kind of surrounding me 24/7 and I wasn't even playing. That's when I decided to lace up the boots again. As an adult it was now my decision to make. Rob was shocked and a little concerned but didn't try to talk me out of it. I was soon doing a pre-season with Collegians in the VAFA. Rob thought it was the best league to dip my toe back in the water. His old Hawthorn teammate James Bennett was the captain.

I remember how excited and nervous I was for my first training session. I thought I was fit. I was wrong and became painfully aware of this about an hour into training. It's not an easy sport to step straight back into after six years of non-playing. Just before the end of the first training session, I broke my thumb. Perfect start. Two weeks later I tore my hamstring. I was woefully out of footy nick after so many years not playing. It was bloody hard work. I soon worked my way in after recovering from the thumb and hamstring, got fitter and was playing A Grade amateurs. The feeling of playing again was exhilarating, and the body, especially the kidney area, seemed to be coping with contact.

Mid-season things took a turn for the worse. During a viciously cold winter training night, I received an accidental knee to my back in a marking drill. I thought absolutely nothing of it. At home later that night I was urinating blood. In that moment, staring at all this blood in the toilet I was overcome with fear. When I left the bathroom and told Rob he was visibly scared, 'Should I call an ambulance?' I told him we should wait till the morning.

He tried his very best to console me, but I was inconsolable. I absolutely thought I was going to lose the kidney. The following days consisted of doctors' appointments and endless tests. Thankfully, the issues caused by the kick in the back were able to be controlled without an operation. It was the final nail in the coffin for me, I was done with any thoughts of playing again. My doctor told me if I ever took to the field again, he would personally run on and physically drag me off. I felt like a complete failure. Consumed again with 'why me?'

Rob proved to be crucial over the next few months in helping to slowly ease me out of my funk. Whenever I was struggling with anything in life, he was the one I would lean on. I reflect on all that now and feel it was another example of me simply trying to at least match what he had achieved. I had genuinely believed that a year or two playing again would result in being picked up by an AFL club. Completely outrageous when I think about it now but back then I was convinced.

Rob was my biggest supporter and kept telling me I would get there eventually once my body re-accustomed itself to the game. He felt if I could actually still play, which was the big question, my chances would be enhanced by the fact he was now embedded with Hawthorn and that they had already shown interest in me years earlier.

When this attempt failed, it was more than just concern about my kidneys, it was something much deeper for me. All hopes of attaining the level he had reached in footy were buried forever. I've rarely spoken about this because it's pointless, wasted air. Even writing about it now still elicits an element of self-pity and sadness within.

Many years later during Rob's infamous speech at my wedding, he admitted through gritted teeth that he thought I might have been a better player than him, if not for me being so sickly. It was a compliment accompanied by a nice little whack. That was his specialty. The velvet sledgehammer approach.

He went on to say that when he first arrived at Hawthorn the recruiters would regularly ask 'how's Pete going?' He started to think they were only interested in him to get to me. Now to put this in context we had bantered back and forth about this for years. I would say 'You know deep down I had you covered, just admit it.' But Rob always had the most brutally swift response, 'Score is on the board mate, how many games did you play?' End of conversation.

To hear him say this on my wedding night was bittersweet. He told me afterwards to delete that part from the wedding speeches DVD, he had a reputation to uphold as the best player in the family. I'm not sure he was joking, so I never did and still have it.

In our home life as kids, Rob was always the one who had me bursting with laughter. The kind of ferocious cackling that would cause any fluid I was drinking to spurt out of my nostrils. It would often take me some minutes to regain my composure and breath. He had an incredible way of making light out of any situation. His sense of humour fuelled us all, especially in the more difficult times. From as early as I can remember, he was anointed the golden child within our family. He was clearly the favourite. Dad would in later years describe him as 'the glue that held us all together.' I'm not sure that is true for all of us, but he was definitely the lightning rod for our family dynamic. Along with Sue, he was the great hope for mum in terms of living the Christian way of life. Sue was not only the eldest but as the only daughter she endured that constant pressure to live up to mum's standards her whole life.

Rob was the one though who went to great lengths not to upset mum in any way. He loved her but feared her opinion of him. We all did to some degree, but it would always cut him to the bone more if mum wasn't happy with him. Mum clearly saw something in Rob and Sue that maybe she didn't quite see in the rest of us. I had always thought Rob was more religious than the rest of us boys, it was patently obvious.

As a teenager he was already into filming and storytelling. He owned a Super 8 camera that would accompany him everywhere. I can still hear the sounds of him splicing up film and the projector playing in the room he shared with Ricky in our Morwell house. He would experiment making short films, funny and very creative. He would wander around interviewing

20

each of us whenever he could. Stupid stuff, silly questions, anything to get a reaction in which he would delight. He was slowly honing skills that would be hugely beneficial in years to come. He loved it, and it was absolutely his favourite hobby growing up.

Our house in Morwell was much larger than our Heathmont abode. It was perfect for such a large family. The only thing slightly questionable was the bizarre kitchen table. It was identical to a booth like you would see in an American diner. It felt like we were in a scene straight out of the sitcom *Happy Days* whenever we sat down for a meal. Four of us squeezed into each side with mum and dad on each end. This is where I'm certain Rob developed what he thought, and we all knew, was one of his biggest flaws. These days it goes by the name of misophonia, which is basically the absolute hatred of anyone eating loudly.

Try cramming eight people into a confined space years on end eating within centimetres of each other and see how that plays out. All of us kids have the noise issue to some degree, but Rob had it the worst. If I ever was foolish enough to attempt eating an apple in the car with him, he would pull over and order me out of the vehicle. True story. There was no chance he would put up with listening to that. He always blamed that *Happy Days* style booth for giving him that affliction. This will go a long way to explaining what we ended up calling our future film production company.

CHAPTER 3

THE NSCA

Before his Hawthorn playing days Rob had joined the National Safety Council of Australia (NSCA) straight out of school. This was a para-military type emergency services organisation based in the Latrobe Valley. It was led by a man called John Friedrich, or Freddo to those who knew him. John Friedrich would years later be found dead with a single bullet shot to the head. Remembered as Australia's greatest fraudster.

This was a defining period in Rob's life and also mine, as a few years later I too joined the NSCA straight out of school. Our first real jobs. In Rob's case he joined immediately after Year 11. The reason he was given this opportunity was because of dad. In early 1980 dad was the Gippsland area manager for a company called Esanda Finance. At the time Esanda had financed several motor vehicles for this small operation called the NSCA. When dad noticed the borrowings had reached $100,000, he decided to have a look at this place called the

National Safety Council to ensure all was above board.

This is where he first met the charismatic John Friedrich. Dad thought the set-up of the National Safety Council was superb. He asked John, 'How do you get a job here?' and John responded, 'Why?' Dad said he had a son in Year 11 who he would love to see get a position with the NSCA. I can only imagine John was trying to keep dad on side as he didn't hesitate in agreeing to employ the Esanda Finance area manager's son. At the end of Year 11 Rob was hired by the NSCA as a cadet. At this stage he had no idea of what his future held, there was no grand plan. His passion and hobby was his camera and creating little films, which was not something that equated to the thought of it being a realistic profession. He went with the flow and the opportunity being laid out in front of him.

As an NSCA cadet Rob was soon training as a fixed wing aeroplane and helicopter pilot. Soon he would be flying helicopters solo. He was still only seventeen years of age. He didn't even have a car licence but could fly aircrafts solo. It was absurd. I remember him taking us on flights and sitting there staggered that he was actually flying a helicopter. It was completely surreal; he wasn't even eighteen years old for God's sake. It didn't help that he would be cracking jokes over the headphones and seemingly not concentrating on keeping us in the air. He was a talented pilot not lacking in confidence. At times he could be a bit of a maverick with how he used the chopper, which would not exactly shock those who knew him. Using company time and expense he would often veer off course and swing by his girlfriend's property to pick her up for dates.

Just land it in the paddocks, say hello to the folks, strap her in and fly off. Normal stuff.

On one occasion he might have taken it a tad too far. Not might have…did. The Latrobe Valley airport where the NSCA aircraft were based at the time, had a drive-in cinema not far from the main airstrip. Playing on the big screen one night was the movie *Apocalypse Now*. Rob could see it in the distance and had an idea.

He had seen the film before and knew about an epic scene where dozens of helicopters are doing a fly-over. When watching this part in the movie you almost feel the helicopters are flying directly at you. Working the night shift, Rob decided to take one of the NSCA helicopters up for a spin.

Circling the drive-in, he descended to a position about five hundred metres behind the screen and hovered in the black of night. Thinking, should I, will I get away with this? he quickly made up his mind. Slowly moving forward he timed his run perfectly. At the exact moment of the epic chopper scene, he lifted the NSCA helicopter slowly up from behind the massive screen and proceeded to do a low fly-over above the parked cars. Mayhem ensued. One of the most epic and frightening things to ever happen at the Morwell drive-in. I'm fairly certain it wasn't legal or within flying regulations, but this was the last thing on his mind as he flew away laughing and thrilled that he had timed it to such perfection. This night is still talked about in hushed tones by those present and still recovering from the bedlam. It goes to the core of who Rob was, never a second thought for consequence, just go for it and worry about any ramifications later.

The problem with all this excitement and the NSCA's unbelievably good working environment was it was built on bullshit. It was all a fraud. John Friedrich had defrauded banks and governments for years to fund the whole operation. I could write a book or make a documentary on this subject alone.

Dad had developed a strong friendship with Friedrich early on through those Esanda dealings. When John asked dad if he would be interested in acquiring the NSCA banking account for the ANZ Bank dad managed to broker a deal based on what he and the bank saw as an unbelievable organisation full of promise and assets. The fact that the NSCA was also doing an excellent job for the community in search and rescue services didn't hurt either. (We always blamed dad for kicking off the whole fiasco…).

When Friedrich asked dad how to deal with the big banks, dad would advise him to 'bring them down to the Latrobe Valley, show them your establishment and all your equipment, give them lunch and then fly them in the helicopters around Gippsland, they won't be anything but impressed.'

Friedrich took this on board and was off and running, honing his scamming skills to expert levels. For many years he successfully secured loans and funding based on the supposed strong financial viability of the company. His amazing interpersonal skills and ability to convince people about anything and everything also helped immensely. From what I understand most of the con was based on assets. An example of this was at our Sale base. He had one container full of the most expensive equipment imaginable surrounded by dozens and dozens of other containers. I remember seeing those containers and having no clue what they were doing there.

John would show prospective financiers one container full of equipment and explain every other container surrounding it was also full to the brim. The problem was they were all empty. There was diddly squat in every other container. As far as I know, not one other person ever knew John was using these containers as a ruse. Remarkably, it seems none of these financiers ever asked to see inside any other container. When dad found out many years later, he was completely stunned, embarrassed, and hurt. It deeply affected him. This was unwarranted in my opinion as he was in the same boat as thousands of others, conned by an expert.

It all came crumbling down in 1989. Friedrich had swindled his way to a $270 million dollar debt. This debt would eventually see the downfall of the State Savings Bank of Victoria. The NSCA collapsed and Friedrich went into hiding. My brother Rob had remained in contact with him over the years and was shocked to receive a phone call from him whilst he was on the run during this period. As Friedrich was considered a fugitive, Rob was now in a position of knowing about the fugitive's possible whereabouts.

Rob was playing at the Hawthorn Football Club at the time so asked his coach, Allan Jeans, what he should do. Allan had previously been a full-time policeman and listened to what Rob had to say and simply responded, 'Robby you cannot defend the indefensible.' With that Rob went into Russell Street police station and told authorities what he knew. Friedrich was eventually located and arrested in Western Australia. He eventually faced court to be charged with more than ninety counts of obtaining property by deception.

He was subsequently found to have entered the country many years earlier from Germany, under the name of Friedrich Johann Hohenberger. Many conspiracy theorists thought he was a spy. Rob who had spent a lot of time with Friedrich over the years never dismissed the theory. Who knows? One thing I do know, regardless of everything else, was that he loved the NSCA, his baby. He looked after his people and had a real passion to ensure the community was kept safe. He gave myself and Rob unbelievable opportunities and experiences which I will never forget. To me it felt like the hole he had been digging got deeper and deeper each passing year and eventually he was too far down to get out. What cannot be dismissed though is the carnage and heartbreak he caused to so many because of his actions.

On 27 July 1991 Friedrich was found dead on his farm with a single gunshot wound to the head. His death was ruled to be suicide. So many questions surrounding this whole episode went unanswered, so many theories of what happened still hang in the air. Rob was firmly of the view he would never have committed suicide. I tend to agree with him.

CHAPTER 4

THE MISSIONARY

It was during his days working as a pilot with the NSCA, that Rob requested a lengthy period of leave to enable time to 'find himself,' as he referred to it. His big sister Sue had recently returned from a couple of years travelling around the world. Sue had been part of Christian missionary organisation called Youth with a Mission (YWAM). Rob was now at the age where he started to look deep inside himself about the direction his life was taking. His strong Christian upbringing and beliefs instilled mainly through mum was front of mind. He had spoken with Sue about her experiences with YWAM and felt this was something he needed to do for himself.

One of the organisation's locations was Hawaii. I was somewhat shocked when he told the family about his plan to go to Hawaii. I thought he was going off on a long holiday and was filthy about it. I wanted to go as well. Six months in Hawaii sounded awesome to me. Plus, he had never been away from home for such a lengthy period and this was something I wasn't looking forward to. We would miss him immensely. You could say dad wasn't overly impressed by the whole idea, I'm certain he thought it was a cult. But mum was thrilled. This would add another dimension to his favouritism in her eyes.

With leave approved from the NSCA, he was soon airborne, this time as a passenger on a Qantas jet flying over the Pacific. After arriving in Honolulu and being serenaded by the hula girls at the airport he made his way to the YWAM headquarters. This trip wasn't a surprise or a shock to those who knew him. Rob had made no secret of his faith. He had lived his life up to that point akin to an angel, if you compared him to most others of his age group. He had never sworn, nor taken a sip of alcohol, or even puffed on a cigarette. It just didn't appeal to him, and he managed to easily dismiss any temptation to do so. The concept of him spending time in a group called Youth with a Mission didn't surprise anyone.

He spent six months immersed in the Christian teachings and lifestyle of YWAM. He was surrounded by like-minded people and loved the experience. We would get regular letters with a Hawaiian postage stamp which I remember looking forward to with much anticipation. To hear of his exploits and be reminded of his humour was very welcome for us back in Morwell. He would send the odd photo as well which clearly showed how much he was enjoying the sun. His tan was something to behold. This always annoyed me. The fourth child was born with the most magnificent olive skin. The fifth child…not so much. I mean, really? That's just plain unlucky. I often think if it had been the other way around, how would he have coped with fair skin? Not great is the simple answer. He was addicted to catching rays. If I was of world class quality in bedwetting, then he was the undisputed world champion of sunbaking. There has never been a more tanned bottom than the one he carried around. Any suggestion from him that he didn't like to sunbathe nude could be quickly shot down in flames, with a mirror produced to show him his own backside. The climate and beaches in Hawaii suited him perfectly, or should I say the climate and nude beaches in Hawaii suited him perfectly.

Near the end of this period of self-reflection, studying the bible, and excessive ray catching, it was time for him to put into place some of the learnings he had acquired by actively working as a missionary. Before he returned home to Australia he was sent to the Philippines. Arriving in Manila, he soon found himself living a far different reality to anything he had known before. With very little access to clean water and any decent food, he began doing missionary work in the heart of the slums and rubbish dumps of Manila.

This was one of the most intense experiences of Rob's life. It stretched him physically and mentally more than anything he had experienced before. This was hell on earth. Overwhelming masses of people living in putrid poverty. The sickness, the stench, the starvation, lack of shelter, the distinct lack of hope, it was as depressing and demoralising as anything he had ever seen. He really had no idea this was the reality of life for so many people across the world.

Alongside a small team of other missionaries, he spent his time preaching the word of God, and trying to help in whatever way he could. One particular night in this place of horror would impact on Rob more than he could possibly imagine.

As he was making his way through the slums late one evening, he could hear screams, not normal screaming but what Rob later described as unearthly. This section of the slums was known for its daily crime and considered a very dangerous place to be at any stage of the day, let alone in the dark of night. The screaming led him to where his fellow missionaries were helping a man in trouble. As he got closer, he realised what was happening, the missionaries were trying to conduct an exorcism on this man. The people surrounding them were yelling that the man was possessed by the devil. The missionaries were trying to hold him down, but he was fighting hard against them, throwing punches, and kicking wildly. Rob stood frozen not quite believing that this was happening right in front of his eyes. He had read and believed in the Bible, including the idea of demonic possession and exorcism. He trusted it to be true. But to see it being attempted made him go weak at the knees. He got up close and did his best to try to help by holding the man's legs down.

What happened next was forever burnt into Rob's consciousness. With the missionaries praying loudly over the man and his violent screaming sounding more sinister, the man started frothing at the mouth. His body was trembling and with a petrifying scream he hissed and spat out huge amounts of saliva. There was a final heavy shudder from the man and then complete peace. He slowly opened his eyes and was more than a little shocked to see the missionaries bending over him. He had no idea what happened. The missionaries were yelling 'Praise the lord.' The onlookers were joyous. They all believed this man had successfully been rid of a demon within. So, too, did Rob. He believed to the core of his being that he had witnessed a spiritual event firsthand.

I've never forgotten Rob telling us this story upon his return. It was like something from a horror movie. Rob was prone to exaggeration...very prone. But this was not an exaggeration to him. It really happened and the memory of that night always haunted him. In his mind he absolutely witnessed an exorcism, and it was very real to him. Many years later when he would battle with his own beliefs, this episode was never far away from his thoughts.

We were thrilled to have Rob back at home once he returned from his travels. Life was so much more enjoyable when he was there. As he was preparing for his return to work after so many months away, the news came in that two of his missionary friends in Manila had been murdered in the slums. He had been with them just one week earlier.

CHAPTER 5

THE HAWKS

Back working in his job as a pilot with the NSCA, Rob had started to get attention from the Hawthorn Football Club. He was being noticed as a pacey wingman playing for the Morwell Tigers in the Latrobe Valley Football League. It wasn't long before the offer to be drafted to the Hawks arrived and a big decision had to be made. Stay in the comfort and stability of his piloting career or take a leap of faith into the footy world which offered no guarantees. Dad was dead against him leaving the security of being a pilot. At this stage Rob hadn't obtained his commercial helicopter licence and dad insisted he do so before considering football. He begrudgingly did what his father requested and stayed on until he was granted a commercial helicopter pilot's licence.

He was more than ready to leave the NSCA as he had started to have doubts about continuing his piloting career. He had endured some frightening times flying over bushfires, and while on various search and rescue missions. He was particularly affected by one incident where he was centimetres away from potential tragedy by flying too close to power lines, his vision impaired by the smoke of a tearaway fire. This was the moment which essentially kicked off the 'yips' with a fear of flying helicopters. He kept on flying after this incident but had definitely lost his confidence. I know this played a huge role in his decision to stop being a pilot and try his hand at playing professional football.

Signing on for his first lucrative contract with Hawthorn, well not exactly lucrative, it was barely a quarter of what he had earned as a pilot, came as a bit of a reality check. But regardless of the lighter wallet, his new career as an AFL player was off and running. The Hawthorn players of the time included some of the all-time greats, Tuck, Ayres, Brereton, Dunstall, Platten etc. I could go on and on. Trying to break into this side was going to be a monumental task. Not only that, trying to keep pace with the extraordinary number of mullets which were in the team was no easy feat. But somehow, with intense perseverance and determination, Rob soon held the mantle of second-best mullet in the club, millimetres behind Gary Ayres. This was a mighty achievement. He loved his hair. His fear of balding could only be described as colossal. I remember him first introducing me to some shampoo he had purchased from hair loss treatment specialists Ashley & Martin.

'Pete, this stuff is magic, it tingles into the scalp. You can actually feel the hair growing stronger.' He had made appointments with A&M (as we used to call them) because he thought he had started to lose his hair. This was unacceptable to him. He blamed the pilot helmets he had worn over the years, adamant the heat combined with sweat and rubbing on his scalp from these helmets was causing issues on his noggin. He would also blame dad who was bald, and both our grandfathers who were bald, and tell me, 'Don't worry it's going to hit you as well.'

This instantly made me petrified. I was losing my hair, too, yet was still in my teens. He would take great delight in inspecting my thatch and telling me I probably had a good twelve months left. We both agreed if ever it came to it, we would absolutely rug up, meaning we would take the plunge into wearing wigs if it became necessary. Not vain at all.

The reality was he hadn't lost any hair, not one strand. It was bountiful up there and his mullet was a thing of beauty. The expensive Ashley and Martin shampoos continued to live in our bathroom and got plenty of use. Don't worry about that.

With his sense of humour and personality Rob became a very popular teammate. He spent most of his days at Hawthorn playing in what he described as the Magoos, which was the seconds. Coach Allan 'Yabby' Jeans used to call Rob the Rag Doll. When he first cast eyes on this spring-heeled young bloke from Morwell, he thought he played football like a rag doll. Many years later I had the privilege of conducting what turned out to be the last interview with Yabby in his aged-care home. It was for my 1971 Grand Final documentary. John Kennedy Senior also came along that day, and it was one of the most glorious few hours I've had making films. I remember Yabby's eyes lighting up when I mentioned the nickname Rag Doll. He spoke with much warmth about Rob.

During his Hawk days Rob also had a part-time role with the AFL in running footy clinics. He was given a car and was out and about each week at various schools across the state. Melbourne Football Club legend Garry Lyon and St Kilda Football Club captain Danny 'Spud' Frawley worked alongside him. Whenever he returned from one of these trips, the car would be covered, absolutely smothered in smashed eggs. Every single time. One night he walked in with egg yolk hard dried on to his face, hair and shirt. He stank. Apparently, he was stationary at some traffic lights when Spud and Garry pulled up beside him on the way back from a clinic. They both let him have it. Dozens of eggs were thrown full pelt in his direction in a fearful two-minute burst. Unfortunately for Rob he had his window down and copped the brunt of it directly.

He adored those days working in the AFL with Spud and Garry. He always said any money he was paid by the AFL for the job was spent purely on eggs. The cars were always returned to the AFL in appalling condition. Imagine pulling up at some traffic lights these days and seeing today's equivalent of Spud Frawley and Garry Lyon in a full-on egg fight on the roads. It would be front page news.

Rob's biggest disappointment while at Hawthorn was when he missed selection for the 1989 Grand Final team, an encounter often described as one of the most epic Grand Finals ever played between Hawthorn and Geelong. Missing out on selection hurt him and left a painful scar within for many years.

In the week leading up to the game he and many of his teammates thought he would be selected, due to a suspension handed out to teammate Peter Schwab in the previous game. Rob arrived at the MCG early on Grand Final morning with his bag in hand, full of nervous energy believing he would be playing. When he entered the rooms his captain, Michael Tuck, approached him and put his arm around him and said, 'Bad luck, mate.'

Rob looked at the whiteboard and noticed his name listed as an emergency. His great friend Greg Madigan had been selected instead. This was gut-wrenching. He tried his best to hide the pain of being a spectator instead of being out on the MCG playing, but it was impossible. The pain was written all over his face as he sat with the crowd in the stands. He was utterly distraught. The weight of this disappointment was the catalyst that drove Rob to succeed from that day on. When he wanted something this badly, he was not going to let anything get in the way. He promised himself he would never feel this way again.

In 1991 he was traded to the Brisbane Bears. He had managed to play seventeen senior games in one of the best Hawthorn outfits of all time, which was a remarkable effort. I'm not sure of the exact number of Magoos games he played for Hawthorn, but it would be in the vicinity of six thousand.

He was a member of the winning Brisbane Bears reserves team in his one and only season with them. He then hung up the boots. This didn't surprise me at all. Whenever he won something we competed in (which was rare) like tennis or golf, he would promptly claim to be world champion and retire on the spot. Never allowing a rematch. I would have to relentlessly beg for him to give me another shot. So, to see him retire immediately after the Bears' reserves flag was standard behaviour. To play even one senior game of VFL/AFL football is monumental. As a family we were so proud of him and the way he conducted himself throughout his entire footballing career. The friendships and relationships he formed over those years were so important to him and for his life to come.

It was during his time at Hawthorn that the seeds were planted for his future filmmaking career. He had begun to do a lot of filming behind the scenes, capturing content. As one of the lads, his teammates had complete trust in him. He had direct access to shoot in and around the club as he pleased. Changerooms, showers, plane trips, bus trips, anything and everything was fair game. The players loved it, especially 'Dipper' (Robert DiPierdomenico) who was honing his own interviewing skills for future network boundary riding duties. Rob must have filmed hundreds of hours of footage over those years although the amount of nudity captured wouldn't be remotely possible in clubland these days.

You could say his first official production was a fly on the wall documentary he created from all this vision called *Good for Football*. He used his own money to produce a VHS version thinking it would sell in its thousands. For the cover insert, he wanted a design which had all the signatures of the players at the time. Let's just say most of those signatures weren't legit. No, better still, let's say all of them weren't legit, except for Rob's. One evening, when he had the original sleeve design ready but still

38

needed the players' signatures before mass printing we took it in turns to delicately sign all the players' signatures on to the sleeve. We based them on a copy of the real signatures we had in front of us. We were chuffed with how real our efforts looked but also slightly concerned how similar they all appeared. If you have one of the eight copies of *Good for Football* sold, take a close look at the signatures, they may look a little dodgy. He also wrote fake reviews on the back of the sleeve. His favourite was, 'A collector's item… — Hawthorn City Council.' He thought it was genius.

Not surprisingly this foray of Robs into the documentary making world didn't exactly fly off the shelves. From memory, the extent of the marketing for the film was a flyer to the Hawthorn membership base. He handed out more than were sold but it never really mattered, he just loved the whole process. The final scene featured himself and Greg Madigan swanning around the Glenferrie Road grandstand naked. Yes, totally naked. Rob's bum was at least ten times browner than the brown and gold coloured seating surrounding them. Imagine players doing that today, and the uproar if that vision was released. No social media back then though…

Regardless of the blatant nudity, it was absolutely unique. A film with footage taken from deep inside the inner sanctum of an AFL club by one of its very own players, who then had the ability to craft a documentary out of it. This would be highly sought after content these days. If ever you get a chance to watch *Good for Football* it won't disappoint. Rob's first real crack (pardon the pun) at a sports documentary of sorts. He was already well ahead of his time.

CHAPTER 6

THE PERFECT STORM

With Rob now residing in Melbourne while plying his trade with the Hawks, life at home became very boring, very quickly. I was now in my teens and only myself and Ricky were still at home. We were now attending St Paul's College in Traralgon, like our elder brothers had done before us. In year 10, I was appointed vice-captain of the school. Here was just another example of where I was close to something Rob had attained before me, but not quite close enough. He was the captain of the school in his day. Still, it was a fantastic honour and something I was very proud of.

The situation at home was rapidly deteriorating. Mum and dad had tried to hold on to this toxic marriage for many years but enough was enough. Dad decided to leave and start a new life in Melbourne. Ricky and I stayed with mum in Morwell. It was an emotional, lonely and traumatic time. I don't blame one more than the other, they both contributed to the mess.

As with many broken marriages, not many people outside the family unit were aware of what was happening on the inside. Mum was revered in the local community as an active member of the church, a primary school religious education teacher, and in many people's eyes a saint. Dad was a highly successful and respected executive with Esanda, as well as a gun sportsman who helped many sporting clubs thrive in the area. The divorce came as a real shock to everyone who knew the family.

Living with a mother who is grieving the end of a marriage is not something I can recommend. As a devout Christian who believed in marriage for life, no matter how tough it might be, she was distraught it had come to this. It has always perplexed me to some degree how long it lasted, as it was not a happy union. Maybe they hung on until the kids were older, but who knows? Part of me thought the separation might give her a new outlook on life, but those first few years after dad left was hell at home. Mum was constantly crying, angry, and leaning heavily on two young sons who emotionally weren't equipped to deal with the situation.

It was around this time when I really started to rebel against the world. It was the perfect storm; the age of sixteen or seventeen a period when that is to be expected to some degree, but a broken home added more spice to the mix. My schooling deteriorated and grades started to drop as I felt completely lost. I began to put zero effort into my education, feeling angry at everyone and everything. Sport was my only real focus, and I was devoting a lot of time to cricket. I couldn't play footy anymore so I was keen on seeing how far cricket could take me.

My eldest brother Graham was very important for Ricky and me during those years. He is ten years older and would drive up from wherever he was living at the time and take us away for surfing holidays. We felt free. My god, those were great times. At the age he was, and living the best years of his life, to take time out for his two younger brothers, whisk them away and be responsible for them is incredible. He wrapped his arms around us and gave us some joyous experiences we will never forget on those holidays. We grew up fast at some of the wild parties he and his surfing mates were regularly involved in. That's for sure. But it never lasted. We always had to return home afterwards, which was depressing. I loved mum and wanted to look after her and make sure she was okay, but when you leave the house and feel as if you've escaped prison, then clearly that's not an ideal environment. It often felt like we had returned to the cell blocks after those trips.

I was rudderless and had no plan for the future. It was mid-year in Year 11 that things changed when dad had arranged a job interview for me with John Friedrich at the NSCA. I wasn't exactly flying as a student, and still annoyed at the world. Everything started to change the minute I walked into Friedrich's office with dad.

It's fair to say I was as toey as a roman sandal. I had met Friedrich numerous times before through Rob and dad's relationship with him and he had been in our home for dinners. It wasn't this aspect I feared. It was more about having no idea of what I wanted to do with my life. My self-esteem wasn't exactly through the roof at the time either. To say I was handed a free hit that day is an understatement. Friedrich greeted us warmly and we sat down. He looked directly at me with those intimidating eyes and asked just one question, 'Pete, why do you want to work here?'

I looked at dad, who was almost willing me with his eyes to answer properly and not blow it. I cannot remember the exact words I spat out, but it was along the lines of how much I loved and respected the NSCA through my firsthand experiences with Rob having worked there. If an opportunity ever arose in the future for me to join the organisation it would be a dream come true.

With that he gave me a wink and said, 'Okay Pete, wonderful. Can you leave me and your dad for a chat, just wait outside.' I was like shit…I blew it. Surely interviews go longer than that. I had wanted to do what Rob had done, to follow in his footsteps and experience life with the NSCA. It felt like I'd stuffed up the opportunity. About twenty minutes later dad and Friedrich came out of the office. John gave me a strong hug and said, 'You are working for me once you finish school this year, welcome aboard.'

I was almost in tears, suddenly I knew what would be happening with my life after school. He then went on with, 'Let's speak again once you finish the year to decide what you will actually be doing here.' He shook dad's hand and was off talking with someone else waiting to see him.

As we were leaving, I asked dad what they had spoken about when I left the office. He told me it was all the usual business stuff, absolutely nothing to do with me until near the end when he told dad, 'Of course Pete can work here, I love your family and look forward to having him here.'

Dad drove me back to school. I remember walking back into the classroom with a grin from ear to ear. I had a job at the end of the year. Not just any job, a job with the NSCA. It was a major moment in my life, a sense of purpose and security I had never felt before. Without question a monumental free hit.

CHAPTER 7

THE TURPS

I was lying in bed knowing it was going to happen at any moment. I'd had this feeling of dread many times during my teenage years and knew it was only moments away, again. Sure enough, it happened. My bedroom door flew open and mum stormed in with an open Bible in her hand.

Only hours earlier she had surprised me by turning up to an event I was attending. It was late in the evening and she caught me red-handed sipping a glass of beer with friends. I was not expecting mum to show up but there she was, and this was the first time she had ever seen me having a beer. The horror on her face (and mine) was palpable. My friends, who knew full well how religious my mum was, went deadly quiet. From the corner of my eyes, I could see them slinking under the table to hide. This was because in my family drinking and smoking were taboo and almost non-existent, except for a few of us sinners. Dad had never drunk or smoked in his life, nor did mum. Neither was acceptable to her as a Christian. Sue was the same, and at that stage Don was forging ahead with his golfing ambitions so I'm not certain he imbibed much back then either. Rob was also a strict non-drinker and remained this way all his life. It was something that never appealed to him.

On the other hand, there was Graham. I don't think there has been a substance of any sort which hasn't been given a good solid hammering by Gray. He lived life to the fullest and was clearly the outcast of the family. But it looked to me like he was having no end of fun. I'm positive the first alcohol I ever consumed was on one of the surfing trips with Graham. He would never let Ricky or I drink much, but you could say he gave both of us a slow introduction to the turps.

When mum caught me having a quiet sip with friends this night, it was a huge shock to her. Later, once home and standing over my bed, she proceeded to read aloud chapter and verse from the Bible, attempting to convince me as to the evils of the drink. To be fair, she always wanted the best for me, especially with my health issues. But this Bible session went on longer than any before. After what must have been at least two hours she finally began to wane, giving up on the sermon because I was drifting in and out of sleep.

This was the moment I decided I had to leave home and get away from this. I know she meant well, but come on. The next day my best mate Steve knocked on the door to catch up and was very sheepish when mum answered. We went to his place to get some relief from the tension in the house and discuss the events of the previous night. I remember having to pause every few minutes so he could regain his composure and stop cramping from laughing so hard. His dad, who was on about his fifth beer for the afternoon and listening in, literally fell out of his chair laughing.

Mum remained bitterly disappointed with me. It felt as if she had abandoned any hope of me living up to her staunch Christian values and walking the path she intended. She had ditched any hopes for Graham and Don by that stage. All she had left was Sue and Rob, and hopefully Ricky who was still very young. The dial on keeping a close eye on me and monitoring my every move was turned up to maximum levels from that day forward.

By then I had started working at the NSCA in administration under an incredible mentor and man called Laurie Wandmaker. This was someone who I viewed as a second father during the first year of my working life. Dad wasn't at home anymore and I was with Laurie every day. He was such a powerful influence and role model for me in my first year of employment. He taught me a great deal about working life, and how to communicate and conduct myself in this new adult world.

An example of his commitment to me was when I turned eighteen. It was time for my test to obtain a driver's licence. I needed a parent/adult to be present with me in the car for the test. Mum wasn't the greatest passenger when I was driving at the best of times, so I didn't want her in the vehicle. Laurie was the only option and he willingly accompanied me in the car with the driving instructor. It sounds like not much of a big deal, but it was to me back then. I have never forgotten him and how important he was to me. I absolutely needed a daily father figure type who was present during those years. He filled that void.

In his wisdom, John Friedrich decided to ease me into the NSCA by working in administration. I was happy to take anything. I had no ambition to be a pilot or jump out of aeroplanes in pararescue. I had no idea what I wanted to do for an occupation, there was a sense it might be something creative but had no clue as to what it was. For my work experience program in Year 10, the school had placed me into a signwriting firm. First day on the job they had me hanging off a ladder about thirty feet in the air painting some filler into a sign. I remember deciding then and there this wasn't for me. Not a great career choice for someone with a raging fear of heights.

Friedrich knew a lot about the Dickson family dynamics through this period. But only now do I think he deliberately slotted me in with Lawrie to help me in more ways than just starting a job. So here I was learning everything in a personnel/ HR environment, strutting around in my green NSCA leather jacket and standard issue pocketknife, with a pager on the belt. The number of times I took the knife out of its pouch or had my pager go off I could count on one hand. Let's just say I wasn't exactly on high alert working in the office. If I wanted the pager to start beeping to look important, I would have to ring it myself, something that might have happened more than a few times. I know full well how I must have looked wearing all the kit and working in administration, prime Leo Wanker type of stuff. Felt good though.

After a year or two with the NSCA in the Latrobe Valley I

felt it was time I moved back to Melbourne. For some reason I had never seen myself staying in the country. I had made some amazing friends in the valley, even met my first long-term girlfriend, let's call her H. But I always had a desire to leave one day and return to Melbourne. I decided to ask if there was any chance for me to get a transfer to our Melbourne office in St Kilda Road. I used to sneak into Friedrich's office regularly and pinch a can of soft drink out of his fridge. Growing up in and around the NSCA and knowing him well meant I didn't really have any fear of the man. I knew full well Rob had cleared the path for me with John. Rob used to give him no end of cheek and got away with it. I used to sidle in even if he was there and quietly help myself to his fridge. He would just smile and abuse me for being a thief (ironic…).

It was in one of these moments when I sat down at his desk and asked him if a transfer to Melbourne would be possible. I told him I was also missing Rob and wanted to be around him more. He stared at me with a curious look for what seemed an eternity before breaking out in a huge grin saying he missed Rob as well. He did have a wonderful smile. I was soon granted a transfer to the NSCA Melbourne office and moved into a house with Rob and my cousin Mal. It felt like pure freedom. Being away from mum and experiencing city life with my big brother and cousin (who I also idolised), were some of the best times of my life.

I began training with district cricket club Melbourne to see if I could make the cut at that level. Cricket was my sporting pursuit now that I couldn't play football. Pre-season was at the

MCG indoor nets during winter, and I remember being a little starstruck when Dean Jones turned up for training. Melbourne was his club. I've never forgotten a run around the Botanical Gardens with the squad on a freezing winter night. Deano had just returned from an overseas tour. I swear he ran the whole way in fluorescent green Speedos. I was in two cricket jumpers and a full tracksuit, and that still didn't feel enough. It was that cold. I put it down to the possibility he might have wanted to show off the suntan he was rocking from his travels. Who knows? I simply remember thinking if this is what it takes to play for Australia, I'm not up to it.

By then, my little brother Ricky had also started working, as an apprentice carpenter in Morwell. A large regret through those years was leaving him as the last one home with mum. I know he felt abandoned by his brothers as well as dealing with the whole divorce. It was such a difficult situation as mum was also going through this feeling of abandonment. For Ricky, growing up in a large family as the youngest child, to then find himself the last one left, I can only imagine how this must have affected him. Today, he is a gun builder running his own business, living in Melbourne with his wife and two beautiful girls. He built my house. I'm so proud of him.

Even though I was glad to be back in Melbourne, I never at any stage felt happy or content in my working life. I tried to do the best I could with the opportunities afforded to me, but administrative type work was not for me.

When the NSCA collapsed, I lost my job. I managed to find a few similar type positions in Melbourne for some big firms.

It was in one of those roles that I became heavily involved in recruitment. This meant interviewing people. I would assess applicants and then go through the whole hiring process. I absolutely loved interviewing. Part of me felt like I had found something that I was pretty good at and, more importantly, even passionate about. Little did I know then what the skills I was picking up interviewing people would do for me a few years later.

CHAPTER 8

YOUR MOVE

Following his football stint with the Brisbane Bears, Rob decided to remain living in Queensland. He had a beautiful new girlfriend called Dusty and life was good. He was completely smitten with this girl. He had first noticed her as he was driving past a farm on his way to football training. Here was this exotic looking girl, blonde hair flowing, taking care of horses. Rob would pull over to try to get a glimpse. He did this probably more times than he really should, probably nudging over the line separating correct normal behaviour from the creepy, stalking type. He eventually built up the nerve to approach her with some lame excuse about hiring horses, or something along those lines. It was all bogus, he only wanted to meet her and introduce the Rob Dickson charm. It must have worked. From that day on, this girl called Dusty who hailed from Zimbabwe and was now living in Australia, was in his life.

The Queensland weather and lifestyle suited him down to

the ground. It enabled the year-long tan! Because he was so popular with the Brisbane team during his playing time, the club approached him to become the official runner under coach Robert Walls. His personality suited the role and he loved to still be around the place. His methods of delivering the messages on game day from the coach to the players on field though, were slightly questionable. An example of his style was evident at the Gabba one day when Rob listened over the phone to Walls causing the paint to peel off the walls. He instructed Rob to deliver a fierce expletive filled message to Brisbane player Jason Baldwin, word for word. Rob trotted out on to the ground in his green polo and shorts and ran directly to Baldwin. He could sense Baldwin was preparing for the worst. Rob delivered the message. 'Mate, just look really angry at me, gesture like I've just given you an almighty spray.' Baldwin did just that while whispering 'Good on you Dicko.' Walls noticed this reaction from Baldwin and when Rob returned to the bench, he picked up the phone to hear Walls saying, 'Great stuff, Dicko.'

He would do the most ridiculous things to keep the team entertained. Some of the players from the Brisbane Lions era still talk about the day Rob stripped off on a Melbourne bridge and took a huge jump into the murky Yarra River that flows through the city. He was unnecessarily retrieving a stray footy which one of them had accidentally kicked over the rails. Totally nude he dived from a fearful height into the Yarra. To add to the drama, it was also a ferociously cold winter's day. Some of the players were convinced he was dead when he didn't emerge for what seemed like an eternity. Eventually he surfaced with a huge grin and Sherrin footy safely in his grasp. This was one of the many impulsive things he would do, often without much thought. And he always, always, came out the other side unscathed.

With income starting to become an issue, he had to turn his attention to what else he was going to do to earn some money. He tried a few different part-time jobs. One involved trying to sell videos via telephone for a video distribution company. This would include newly released movies that needed to be stocked on the shelves. Things got interesting when a new porn title was released, and he had to spruik the benefits of having the film in stock.

But there was really only ever one thing on his mind in relation to what he wanted to do with his life, he wanted to be a filmmaker. He was living in Mermaid Beach on the Gold Coast during this time. One of his good mates in the area was Trevor Hendy, one of Australia's most popular ironmen. Together they discussed making a film about health and safety in some form. Trevor with his lifeguard passion and Rob with his background in the NSCA, as well as being a budding filmmaker, made for a perfect union. Thus *Your Move* was born. Their idea was to make a unique emergency life-saving adventure film. Something which would teach the basics of emergency life support.

In order to get this project off the ground Rob set up a company called Health & Safety Australia. The challenge was then to fund the project. Rob was on a mission to get investment. Without any experience in making a film of this nature, this was no easy task. His method was to relentlessly approach wealthy individuals all over Australia to garner interest in the project. He devoured *Business Review Weekly* (the BRW magazine) to see who was on the rich list and then contacted them with more front than Myer's.

With his persistent drive and personable manner, he eventually landed some big fish and secured funding for the production. But sourcing the funding turned out to be the easy part. He now had to make a film. With zero experience in producing and directing a film of this nature, with actors and large crews, it was a real baptism of fire. The only way was to learn on the job. Through his intense passion he made it happen.

He always said that experience was worth years of studying filmmaking as he was right in amongst it, hands on each day while having the added responsibility of being in charge. With Trevor Hendy prominent on-screen within the film, they hoped it would get traction nationwide in schools. The school program was a terrific package and very well done for its time. Unfortunately, it didn't really take off as well as they hoped. Rob put it down to First Aid not being sexy enough.

They had also wanted something practical to accompany the film so the *Your Move* First Aid Kit was created in unison with the school package. From memory Rob had swung a deal somewhere in China to mass produce these kits. Convinced they would sell in their thousands he was highly excited when the shipment arrived. It was a bold and courageous attempt to fill stores Australia wide with this new product, but again sadly it didn't take off as he expected. Hundreds of kits ended up gathering dust and were never sold. I still have a bunch of them somewhere, possibly now a little unusable. He would always say, 'At least I'm having a crack.' I loved that.

It was during this time that we had started discussing how we should one day work with each other. I was fascinated by what he was up to, missed being around him and hated the work I was doing. When I witnessed what he was creating with *Your Move* and the enjoyment he had making the film, I wanted to be a part of all that. I knew his talent, trusted his abilities, but the only problem for me was I was in stable and high earning employment. It would be an enormous risk to let that go and take on a partnership with your brother, with no guarantees of being successful. I also didn't want to simply work for him, I wanted to be an equal partner in whatever we undertook. How would I do this? When would I do this?

The answer to these questions arrived on a sunny Saturday in August 1997. Everything going on in my world was flipped on its head with the purchase of a twenty-four game Tattslotto ticket.

CHAPTER 9

ONE IN EIGHT MILLION

'Think I might just zip over to the newsagent,' I said to my then medical student girlfriend, Ness. She had parked her car in Smith Street, Collingwood. We were en-route to Echuca for the weekend to catch up with some friends but took a quick stop to return a video to the rental store. They were in vogue back then. Ten seconds earlier I had noticed a newsagency window advertising that evening's Tattslotto draw, worth five million dollars.

As we left her red Ford Corsair, also in vogue back then, I mentioned I was going to grab some orange juice, a newspaper and a Tatts ticket from the newsagent.

'Do you want anything?' I asked.

'Juice and I'll have a Tatts ticket as well,' she replied.

Although I cannot remember her handing me any money to pay for her ticket, she assures me she did. I'm inclined to believe her because Ness was one fiercely independent soul who insisted on paying her way with most things. We had been going out for about sixteen months. We first met at sub-district cricket club Malvern, where I was playing alongside her elder brother Dave. Even though our relationship was only in its second year, I was already having thoughts that she might be the one. I had strong feelings for her. We just seemed to click.

While Ness returned the video, I stood impatiently waiting in line for the counter at the newsagency. I hate lining up, always have. I remember getting really annoyed by the older woman in front of me taking forever to decide how many tickets she wanted. She finally decided to buy ten quick picks, and then proceeded to pay in coins. I always seem to be behind someone like this in a queue. I do remember thinking ten quick picks was a fair crack at it though, good for her.

When I finally made it to the counter I promptly ordered two twenty-four game tickets. I thought those behind me would be super impressed by how quickly I had ordered, paid and departed. As I was leaving I looked around for some acknowledgement for not holding them up, but not one person was even remotely paying attention.

When I made it back to the car Ness gave me the standard, 'What took you so long?' I mentioned the old love and her coins to get me off the hook. As we drove away, I had a ticket in each hand. I started waving them around spouting, 'Now which one is the winner, which is the lucky ticket?' on repeat, thinking I was hilarious. As I chose one and slipped the other ticket into the car console, I kept bleating on, 'Being the kind of generous guy I am, when my ticket wins the five million, I will give you one million, a fifth of the winnings.' Ness agreed she would do the same if her ticket won. We laughed it off and completely forgot about it as we enjoyed our weekend away.

By Sunday afternoon we were back in Melbourne having returned from our trip. I was living in the suburb of Richmond with friends in a shared house at this stage. Ness had decided to stay over and go straight to university from there on the Monday morning. As we were lounging about watching some TV, one of my housemates told us he was checking his Tattslotto numbers. This prompted Ness and I to do the same, forgetting we had them in our pockets. I asked my housemate to read out the numbers slowly as we checked. My ticket proved to be a complete dud. I screwed it up and threw it away in disgust. Ness then asked for the numbers to be read out a second time. I noticed she was showing an unusual amount of interest in her ticket. She casually mentioned that on the last line of her quick pick, there appeared to be a bunch of the numbers. I leaned over her shoulder to look at her ticket while listening to the numbers again. Our attention was glued to the bottom line. One after the other, the correct numbers were being called out. It got to the fifth correct number, and I was kind of numb thinking, 'No way.' When we heard the final number, we just froze. The bottom line of a twenty-four game quick pick had all six numbers drawn. You are in a situation where you just don't believe it, so we checked another ten times at least, but it was accurate. We had a 24-game Tattslotto quick pick that on the bottom line had all the correct six numbers drawn. We sat there stunned, then began jumping around celebrating like anyone would do when they had just won the lottery.

That night we didn't sleep a wink. Our minds were spinning out of control. I was petrified something might happen to the ticket overnight. Ness was a world champion at misplacing things. It was a modern miracle she hadn't lost the ticket over the weekend. We weren't registered Tattslotto players so if we lost the ticket, we lost the win. We put it under the pillow between us for the whole night. The other thing keeping us awake was in those days you had to wait until the Monday following a Saturday draw, to know how many winners there were, and thus how much you had won.

At this point it felt like we had both won Tattslotto, but the reality was Ness had the winning ticket. The one I put in her console the day before was the winning quick pick. Without any discussion, we seemed to stick to the verbal deal of whoever won would give a fifth of the winnings to the other. My only thought at that stage was how lucky I was that I even offered that deal, otherwise, I'd be getting zilch.

We had no clue if we had won five million, one hundred thousand, or even fifty cents. All sorts of scenarios were playing out in our heads. With no sleep we were up early, Ness left the ticket with me and took off to attend something she couldn't miss at university. I then made a phone call to Tattersalls to see what the process was if you had a winning ticket. They instructed me to take it into Tattersalls' head office and present it there. I sensed the person on the other end of the telephone was somewhat sceptical.

I called Ness and told her the situation and how I would pick her up in an hour or so and we would venture into Tattersalls.

From memory I drove about as slowly as my mum did many years earlier returning me from hospital. Absolutely petrified to have an accident and maybe somehow lose the ticket. I must have caused utter havoc on the roads. We entered Tattersalls full of anticipation. A friendly woman welcomed us and said, 'How can I help you?'

Ness proudly stated she thought we had a winning ticket. The woman broke into a huge smile and eagerly asked for the ticket to scan and confirm. As the ticket entered the scanner, the monitor started blasting out with all the bells and whistles. Confirmation. We had won first division. It was at this point I started to tremble a little, asking how many winners there were. She checked her screen and told us, 'There are five first division winners.'

It took a moment to register. This meant one million dollars. Considering the worst-case scenarios we envisaged the night before, trying to convince ourselves we'd still be happy no matter how many winners there were, this was incredible news. Sure, just being the sole winner would have been nice but one million dollars, who could possibly be upset about winning such an amount? It was momentous. We hugged for what seemed like forever. Once all the paperwork was completed, we left relieved it was now official, floating and speechless. Two weeks later a $1 million cheque from Tattersalls arrived in Ness's mailbox. I mean, an actual $1 million cheque. It was absurd. This was a phenomenal amount of money for the time.

During those next few weeks things started to get a little dicey. We had begun to share the news with family and close friends. The problem started to emerge when opinions were being strongly floated to me that I should in fact receive fifty per cent of the win. I had purchased the ticket and some stupid jokey mention of one fifth shouldn't remain in stone in such a situation. This was predominately coming from my family and friends. Rob was particularly vocal and wanted me to sort it out with Ness.

On the reverse side, Ness's family and friends thought it was all perfectly legitimate and should remain split according to our deal. It's not hard to imagine the friction beginning to bubble under the surface, especially from me and my family. Ness appeared comfortable with everything as it stood. Fair enough too. We were still a relatively new couple. Who knew what the future held? I understood her position.

We discussed it at length. I knew Ness was under a lot of pressure from her family to keep the status quo. All I will say about the outcome is that I received much more than a fifth from her. This detail remains between us.

We gave a large proportion of the money away as gifts to our families. I'm not proud to say we bought matching Saab cars, mine blue and hers green. We also managed to each buy our first properties. It seems ludicrous but even this amount of money soon starts to dwindle very quickly. But it still meant we were now financially secure. Whether this be together or not, we were in an extremely solid position for the future.

I look back now and wonder how we stayed a couple after the win. When money and family issues collide it's never easy. Thankfully, we managed to get through it all. Today we are happily married (well at the time of writing anyway...) with three beautiful kids, forever grateful. My recommendation for Tattslotto is buy a ticket, who knows what can happen. Or ask me to buy you a ticket...

What would I have done if I had chosen my right hand instead of the left when holding the two tickets? I would have split it fifty/fifty without hesitation. No doubt. I've never been frugal with money, something my wife would well attest to. But being the person who bought the tickets and beat the one in eight million odds will do me.

CHAPTER 10

HUSH PRODUCTIONS

'Pete, just listen to me…this is the best idea ever…what if you took $2000 out of your winnings, give me $1000, and we take a trip to Crown Casino? Whatever profits we make we split down the middle fifty/fifty. I will turn my $1000 into at least $10,000 so it's a win-win!' One hour later I'm in the bank withdrawing $2000 from my account. From there I drove to Crown Casino with an excited and extremely optimistic brother sitting in the passenger seat.

Rob was very persuasive when he wanted to be. Unbeknown to me at the time he was in the midst of a little gambling phase back in Queensland. He told me this a few years later and it all made sense to me thinking back on his manic behaviour that day. He wouldn't lose too much money during his sojourns to the Gold Coast casino, as he didn't have a lot of money to lose, but it was still a side to him I had never expected. As part of his strong Christian values when growing up, gambling was considered taboo. It surprised me he had ventured into this area, but it was during a time where he wasn't earning much. The lure of winning some cash to help in that regard, briefly took hold of him. Thankfully, it didn't last too long before he made the decision to just stop, go cold turkey. But I don't think the desire for a big financial win was ever far away from his thoughts.

So, there we were, storming our way into Crown Casino. Rob was in Melbourne for a visit and was more than a little caught up in the excitement of the recent Tatts win. We arrived at the casino, with Rob telling the security guard at the entrance how we might be needing a truck to be backed in to take away our winnings. I'm sure they haven't heard that one before, I thought. This was the kind of confidence levels Rob was rolling with. Without going into detail about the bets we placed, we must have looked like two toddlers who had guzzled on red cordial and were charged up to the extreme. Within minutes, with the sugar hit over, the tantrums arrived. Barely fifteen minutes later, we were exiting the casino floor out of cash. As we walked by the same security guard on the way out, I quietly informed him we might not need that truck after all. He gave us both a smirk.

This was Rob though, impetuous and convincing, to me anyway. Within a few hours we were cringing at how pathetic we were at gambling. I blamed him and he blamed me. Even though this can only be put down as a massive failure, for some reason it is a treasured memory. I think it's because whenever I could spend time with him, it didn't matter what we were doing, it was then that I seemed to feel at my happiest. He knew me better than anyone else. He understood me more than anyone else. We were brothers, of course, but also great friends. I can comfortably say he was the best friend I had in my life. Therefore, when it came to making the decision to join him in his little business venture it was a no-brainer. However, before I officially invested into the business of Health & Safety Australia I remember flying one of my best mates, Ian Thorn (an accountant), up to Queensland with me to check over the books.

'What do you want me to tell you if I think his business is a bust?' he said on the flight up.

'What are you getting at?' I responded with a smile.

'Well, let's be honest, is this a pathetic attempt to convince yourself it's the right thing to do, even though you have already made the decision?'

He was right. I only wanted to look like I was ticking all the boxes with Rob and taking the brother element out of the decision. The business had no real assets and there was nothing locked in going forward other than Rob's enthusiasm, so financially it was never going to be a smart investment. But I wasn't giving that any credence, I wanted to be partners and see what the future would hold for us. When Ian finished looking over the books, which took him approximately three minutes, I shook Rob's hand and we were in business together.

One of my strong recollections of those first few months working with Rob was when he managed to organise an appearance on a morning television program, hosted by Australian TV legend Bert Newton. He flew to Melbourne with Trevor Hendy, I picked them up from the airport and we drove into the television studios. Trevor was to be interviewed by Bert about *Your Move* and try to promote sales of the package. I was a little excited, I must admit. I'd never met Bert Newton and was looking forward to doing so.

In the car, Rob was in his element describing to us in specific detail the current 'rug' Bert was rolling with. 'Rug' meaning Bert's wig. Rob always thought he was the foremost authority on wigs. He used to state he could easily spot one from a thousand yards. This didn't help me at all when I was first introduced to Bert behind the cameras in the studio. He was a complete gentleman and very polite when greeting us. The problem for me was that Rob was standing directly behind him and in my eyeline, gesturing to the wig and making sure I was noticing. This was his standard move to embarrass me in most things we both thought funny. He would discreetly wind me up and I would lose it while he remained Mr Innocent in the background. I vainly attempted to hold it together but failed miserably and broke into hysterics, face to face with the great man, Bert. I looked like an imbecile. I'm sure Bert thought I was a raging halfwit. This was my first meeting with television royalty. Rob was very happy with himself indeed.

During the segment with Bert and Trevor the 1800 phone number appeared on screen for viewers to place their orders. Rob and I were taking guesses at precisely how many were being sold as this was happening, one hundred, one thousand, maybe even five thousand. We were chock full of confidence it would be a huge result. The next day we received the much-anticipated call from the network informing us of the total sales. We had sold three. Yes, that's correct, three. Still, I got to meet Bert, so it wasn't all bad.

With the *Your Move* school program and first-aid kit package dying a slow death, my first year or so was not exactly a financial success, the complete opposite in fact. Rob was still operating out of Queensland and I was in Melbourne, so any proper working processes were non-existent. We did produce what we thought would be a product that would change the world — a hip and knee replacement video. With the help of orthopaedic surgeon Peter Wilson, we ventured into the world of orthopaedics. This instructional video provided an explanation of what the surgery entailed, with recovery and rehabilitation advice. Our marketing consisted of putting an advert in an over-fifties' weekly newsletter. Surprisingly, it didn't really take off. Even though we thought it was innovative, the demographic we were targeting didn't really like the idea of purchasing a video, as well as coughing up the steep costs of seeing a surgeon. So that made for a swift end to any medical film production ambitions.

I wanted Rob to relocate to Melbourne. If we were going to make a go of this, we had at least to be in the same State. He had only recently married his beautiful Dusty. The wedding took place in Zimbabwe. I was the best man and Ricky was a groomsman. The whole trip and experience in Zimbabwe was incredible. One of the more memorable moments was when Rob took Ricky and I bungee jumping at Victoria Falls. At the time it was known as the highest bungee jump in the world and I am scared shitless of heights. It was located on the Victoria Falls bridge, the crossing point between Zimbabwe and Zambia. It was one hundred and eleven metres high. Annoyingly, Rob and

Ricky looked completely at peace and even eager to jump off the bridge. I could barely look over the edge. When the time came for them to strap me into the ankle harnesses, I thought I was going to vomit everywhere. Rob was filming and taking much delight in how scared I was. As I stood on the precipice about to launch into what I thought was my last moments on earth, I was unaware Rob had worded up the bungee operators to add a little spice as I leapt off the rails. So here I am being yelled at with the instruction to 'go go go' ... so I went...about two feet into my swan dive I heard the operators yelling 'wait wait! Come back, come back, come back!'

I am still amazed how I didn't have a heart attack and die mid-dive. Rob had struck. The next five minutes were harrowing. Thankfully, the bungee straps held and I bobbed up and down dangling a hundred metres below the bridge. You then had to wait mid-air swinging wildly until an operator is winched down to grab you and take you slowly back up. Very slowly back up. It was nothing but torture. How anyone does this for fun is beyond me. All I could hear as I got closer to the bridge while clinging madly to the operator, almost choking him with my grip, was Rob laughing so hard he could have burst a lung.

I remember being sad to leave Zimbabwe and return home to Australia. Rob and Dusty were staying on for a while and he dropped me off at Harare airport for the flight home. After checking in and walking with me to the customs area, he waved me off saying his goodbyes. The Qantas jet was already on the tarmac, so boarding wouldn't be too far away.

I was wandering around the gate lounge looking for a snack

bar without success when I heard the shouting 'Pete, come with me.' I looked around and it was Rob. He had somehow snuck through the customs gate without a ticket and was urging me to follow him back out. I was saying, 'What the hell are you doing? I'm about to board, I can't leave here.' He wouldn't take no for an answer and was telling me that I had to see something before I flew out. Harare airport back then was not large and relatively easy to get in and out of security wise. We departed the terminal, jumped back into his car, and drove out of the airport. All this while my flight was only minutes away from boarding.

I was looking at him like he had gone completely mad. He was trying to reassure me with, 'This will be worth it, trust me.'

Not far from the airport, he pulled over to the side of the road and slowly drove into some bushland. As he brought the car to a halt, I looked out the front window and there was an elephant staring right at us. It was standing two metres in front of the car with some baby calves close by. Rob was beside himself saying, 'How good is this?'

I was mightily impressed, I must admit. We were only metres away from these magnificent beasts. But this sublime moment lasted for literally a moment. It then turned ugly. Fearfully ugly.

As we were sitting there, very happy with ourselves, admiring the scene in front of us, mumma elephant looked directly at these two imbeciles and decided they were too close for her liking. She charged. I looked at Rob and it's the only time I'd ever seen raw panic in his face. This caused me to panic. I started yelling, 'Reverse, reverse' he was yelling, 'I'm trying!'

It took what seemed like forever for him to get the car into reverse gear, when in reality it was probably seconds. He put his foot to the floor, and we were reversing as fast as the car would go. He wasn't even looking behind at where we were going, we were both too focussed on the elephant charging and seriously catching up with the car. I thought this is it. This is how we die, trampled by an elephant. Nice one. Imagine getting to heaven and they check you in and say, 'Hello my son, and why are you here today?' and you have to answer with, 'Well funny story … I was supposed to be on an aeroplane but instead decided to go and get up close with an elephant, and unfortunately, we were trampled by said elephant.'

Thankfully, I didn't make it to the gates of heaven this day. The only reason we were spared being crushed by an elephant, was because it took sympathy on us and decided to stop the chase. I can only think she felt pity. Plain old-fashioned pity after noticing our faces through the car window. We drove back to the airport without saying a word. Not one word. Still visibly in shock, we could barely nod at each other as I exited his car. I shuffled inside the terminal and made my way to the boarding gate looking what could only be described as dishevelled. If there had been any decent security in place I would have been pegged as a nervous drug runner. Never have I been more relieved to sit myself down on an aeroplane ready for take-off.

Not long after our elephant expedition Rob and Dusty were back in Australia and making the big decision to relocate from Queensland to Victoria. This was exciting for me as we could now really knuckle down and try to make a go of this business partnership. We also decided to change the Health & Safety Australia company name so we could spread our wings into other areas.

We brainstormed potential business names to kick off our new venture. As mentioned, Rob had severe noise issues. When we lived together, we would go to the cinema once a week to watch the latest flicks. We loved watching movies. The problem for Rob was this would take place in a cinema, where people would generally eat food. It was an element of the movie watching experience which Rob could never get his head around. 'Who would possibly want to eat in a cinema? You are there to watch a film, it's not a restaurant,' was his oft voiced opinion.

For me, it became more about watching Rob during a film than actually watching the film. He would be on constant alert in case anyone in the vicinity had the temerity to eat something. If he heard the slightest chip bag sound or, God help us, a soft drink slurp, we would have to move to seats as far away as possible from the culprits. The record for the number of times we moved during a single movie was eleven. It was at the Balwyn Cinema, and I remember it vividly. There was barely a section of the seating we didn't visit. He was infuriated at nearly everyone in the cinema, I've never laughed harder.

I'm not exactly sure why, but we threw this quirky little noise issue into the mix of potential business names. We started to brainstorm options around the fact people should ideally not eat loudly, especially at the cinema. We discussed many stupid options like Shoosh, Be Quiet, Tone it Down, Muzzle It, this type of theme. After getting nowhere fast I suggested the possibility of Hush. Rob instantly loved it.

Right then and there, we decided to name our business Hush Productions.

CHAPTER 11

THE PASSION TO PLAY

'This is perfect, perfect,' Rob exclaimed as we inspected a commercial office rental near the Yarra river in Richmond. 'It seems an awfully big space for just the two of us,' I mused, but he was having none of it. 'Nah we will need it,' he said with a smile, making me think he believed we would be expanding fast. The agent appeared pleasantly surprised by how keen we looked and thrust the official lease papers in front of us for signing. Prone to rash decisions, we signed immediately on the dotted line. This was now the official home of Hush Productions Pty Ltd. As the agent drove off, I had a sense he was thinking … suckers.

To get any serious projects off the ground we had to at least start looking like a professional outfit, and that included having a proper set-up. We now had the office space, which was nice, but we desperately needed work to pay for it. This is where my faith in Rob and trust in his vision for Hush was confirmed.

He was adamant and very bullish our future lay in the

production of sports documentaries. The first one should be in his lane, an AFL football documentary. In those days, Australian-made sports documentaries were rare. There had been a few good ones made, but not many.

'Great,' I said … and after a few more seconds, 'How?'

The very next day we walked into the offices of the AFL Players' Association (AFLPA). Its CEO at that time was Andrew Demetriou, who would soon become the CEO of the AFL. Rob had a very close friendship with Andrew through their playing days together at Hawthorn. Rob had contacted him for a catch-up to discuss this doco idea, and Andrew invited us into his office. As we sat in the AFLPA offices, which were then located in the heart of the city, Rob explained his vision to Andrew. It would be a unique and personal insight into the experience of playing the game at the highest level, directly from those who knew it best, the players.

Andrew loved the idea and concept. The AFLPA was soon on board with supporting us in access to players and making a commitment to help launch the film once completed. It would not, however, be contributing any funding. It was up to us to find an investor to back the film.

Those were the days when investing into locally produced films of this nature could entitle investors to some tax relief and so we were hopeful of attracting at least some interest.

As we were leaving Andrew's office, I remember him introducing me to one of the women on the staff, saying, 'This is Pete, he is very weeaaallltthhyyyyyy' in his typical loud drawl. I cringed and pressed the elevator button furiously to get out of there. Rob must have worded Andrew up on the Tattslotto situation and he found the whole thing fascinating. He took great joy in my reaction. Rob laughed all the way down in the elevator.

When we reached the street, with Rob's filthy unroadworthy VW Beetle parked out front, we noticed a parking ticket nestled under the windscreen wipers. Rob casually took the ticket and placed it on another nearby car's window. This was his standard move whenever he received a parking ticket. His theory was that no one ever actually checked the ticket properly. 'They only ever look at the amount to pay,' he said. I shudder to think how many innocent people paid for Rob's parking tickets over the years.

We had set a budget of one million dollars for the production. It would be a two-year project involving interviewing nearly two hundred past and present VFL/AFL players. It was a massive undertaking for two brothers new to the world of documentary making.

Thankfully, with a lot of help from associates who knew more about the intricacies of trying to raise money than us, we eventually found and secured investment for the film. This was monumental. We had absolutely no idea what we were doing, but at least we were off and running with our first Hush Productions documentary, *The Passion to Play*.

Rob was the key creative, the writer, editor, producer, and director. Not much on his plate. My role in the beginning was line producer and production/office manager of sorts. We had a good friend of mine, Robert Welch, looking after our accounts including budgets and general finance. After hiring camera and sound freelancers we had a lean mean team ready to go.

We began by calling a huge database of players to try to slot in interviews. It was much easier back then to line up players for interviews. Managers and clubs were nowhere near as protective of players as they are today. It was as simple as giving the player a direct call, hoping he would agree to be part of it, then sorting a time and place that suited for an interview.

Most, if not all, of those approached were delighted to be involved. I put this down to the fact they knew it had AFLPA support and because Rob was the director and was known and trusted by players across the football landscape.

We learnt on the run. Trial and error. A lot of errors. It was stressful yet enormous fun. Watching Rob interview players, listening to story after story, holding the boom microphone where necessary, learning all facets of the production game was thrilling to me. It really felt like I had finally landed in the type of work that suited me and I was passionate about. I was thriving in the environment and process of making a film, while having a front row seat to Rob's style of crafting a story together.

His easy-going manner and personality meant the players would instantly be at ease and let their guards down. The interview content gathered during this production was astounding, mainly because of the raw honesty captured. We would always drive away from interviews with Rob asking, 'Was that any good?'

I would often be shaking my head saying, 'So good, not sure what you can leave out.'

This was the first time I really noticed self-doubt within Rob. He would always appear to have this inner confidence that everything was under control, but during the early days of this production he was anything but self-assured. I would come to learn that self-doubt is a crippling element of directing a film, for me anyway.

It was proving hard enough for us to keep pace with the requirements of a production of this magnitude without extra drama being thrown at us. But, sure enough, extra drama was being thrown at us. The offices of Hush Productions were being burgled regularly, at least once every two weeks. Where we were located proved to be a magnet for the smash and grab types. I could see now what might have made the agent so keen to sign us up. We had the building fitted with alarms and I was getting phone calls from the security firm, often somewhere between 2 and 4 am with, 'Sorry mate — the alarm has gone off at the premises.'

The big stress factor for us was that we had all our equipment including very expensive cameras, computers, edit suites, everything needed for film production, all stored there. Our interview tapes, all the footage acquired, it was all there for the taking. We had strict targets to make for the investment drawdowns and responsibilities to the investors so we couldn't afford to fail. It was petrifying.

Whenever Rob and I shared premises, whether it be a house or, as in this case, an office building, we simply never had any luck. We were always being broken into. In one house we shared years earlier, we were robbed six times in five days. The problem back then was Rob refused to lock doors. He would waltz out of the house and leave the front and back doors and windows open with gay abandon. It drove me nuts. It also attracted the thief element like a red rag to a bull. Every time the police came they would be baffled by the fact there seemed to be no signs of any forced entry. Rob would say to them, 'Geez, they must be good,' insinuating that we were being targeted by criminal masterminds. It was hard to keep it together when he trotted that out, especially as I knew he was trying to make me laugh in front of them.

So, when we started to get robbed regularly in our Hush offices, it was hard not to point the finger at a certain someone. Fortunately, we managed to survive without too much damage and loss of property. We invested in safes and locked most things down and this seemed to work. But I'm not sure it made any change to Rob's inability to lock doors.

One of Rob's old teammates and good friend, Peter Schwab, was now the coach of Hawthorn and recruited his good mate back into the club as the runner. This gave Rob some incredible inner sanctum access for filming, which would be of huge benefit to our film. It was while at the club one day that he decided to insert a tiny camera into a football. He built this peculiar little camera contraption and placed it inside a Sherrin football after removing the bladder. We were able to use this for action shots not seen before in AFL football. Shots such as two ruckmen competing for a tap out with the camera/ball flying directly down to their hands, players running along and collecting the ball off the ground, receiving it in a handball, kicking to each other and other moments, all 'seen' from the football's perspective.

This device was not exactly made to world-class standards, but it did what we needed it to do. The tiny set-up inside the hollow ball would dismantle in an instant if not carried correctly, or bumped too hard, but it worked. I thought it was brilliant and gave the viewer rarely seen angles of action. Rob would also wear a hidden mic and camera while doing duty as a runner during real games. He would collect vision up close and personal on field, in amongst the players as a game was being played. This was well before steady cams and the like were introduced to grounds.

Hearing the up close and personal sounds of the game captured from his hidden mic was also ground-breaking at the time. His role as official runner allowed him an access that could not be gained otherwise. It also meant he spent far too much of his time out on the field trying to capture the action instead of doing the job he was meant to be doing — delivering messages for the coach. It was all highly out of order as he hadn't even told the club he was doing it most of the time, let alone informing the AFL. But this was Rob, take the risk and worry about being hauled over the coals later.

The most controversial part of the film was a re-enactment of an infamous training session the Brisbane Lions conducted in 1991. One of the past players interviewed for the film was an ex-Brisbane Lions player Shane Strempel. He emotionally recounted the story of when he was asked by his then coach Robert Walls to don the boxing gloves and stand in the centre of a circle surrounded by his teammates. As part of this punishing training session, Strempel had to face up to teammate after teammate who would take turns in entering the circle to box against him. They each belted the living daylights out of him and the session only ended when one of the players demanded it be stopped before Strempel was killed.

Rob was very keen to show the re-enactment of this as an overlay while Strempel was telling the story. He directed the shoot on a cold and wet night at Glenferrie Oval with a bunch of VFL players. It looked eerie and brutal on screen. Rob had given Robert Walls a call during the crafting of the film to explain he was going to tell this story. Walls didn't really have a problem with it at the time from my understanding. But once the documentary was released and he viewed the way Rob had shot the piece, he was furious. He thought it was completely over the top in its portrayal and was filthy at Rob. I don't think he ever spoke to him again, although I can't be sure.

This affected Rob deeply. He hated thinking anyone had a problem with him, and he hated the fact he might have stepped over the line with trust gained from his time with Robert Walls in Brisbane. He liked to be liked. This incident was also where I first witnessed the fine line you must tread when making documentaries. Decisions are constantly made to add emotion and impact to the storytelling, for which ultimately you as the director must take responsibility.

After nearly two years of work, we finally completed *The Passion to Play*. Rob had in my eyes created a masterpiece. Nearly two hundred past and present players were interviewed, and their stories were told to perfection by Rob. It was released in stores on a double pack VHS. Yes, correct, the old double pack VHS. Eventually it made it to DVD, but the VHS version was first off the production line. The AFLPA put on a gala cinema night in Chadstone to launch the film. Many of the players were there along with all the AFL heavyweights.

I sat at the back of the cinema with Rob as the guests took their seats. I was so proud of what he, and we, had achieved together, as well as everyone who helped us along the way. He looked at me and said, 'We did it.'

The curtains rolled back and our first sporting documentary made as brothers began to roll on the big screen. I sat there praying the moment wouldn't be ruined by someone opening a pack of chips or daring to start munching on popcorn. I wanted Rob to remain in a good headspace ... and his seat.

CHAPTER 12

SURVIVOR

There were many things we had in common as brothers and the love of the television series *Survivor* was high on the list. We were well and truly hooked on watching the US version of the show.

One day during the months after *The Passion to Play* release, Rob wandered into the office to tell me had applied to appear in the first Australian version of *Survivor*. He had made a little video of himself and sent in his application hoping he might get a shot. I kind of laughed it off thinking 'Good luck.' Jobs weren't exactly flying in through the Hush doors.

We were plodding along with the odd corporate video and trying to find our next big documentary project. After getting Hush off to a roaring start we were soon brought back down to earth with the realities of this business. It's hard. Really hard. When there are no projects coming in, you are not getting paid.

So when Rob noticed an advertisement showing Channel

Nine was going ahead with the first *Australian Survivor* series with a very attractive $500,000 purse for the winner, he couldn't resist applying. It would be unheard of if he won. It would mean two brothers had each hit the jackpot by winning large sums of money. You could get any odds you wanted on this ever happening to two people in the same family and this spurred him on even more.

I viewed his application video and thought it was well done, which was no surprise. He obviously had the looks, which helped, and showed his great sense of humour on screen. Also he was an ex-AFL player, something I thought might really appeal to the producers.

As it turned out, it did.

'You cannot tell anybody.' It was 10 am on a Tuesday when Rob burst into the office bubbling with excitement. Initially I was shocked he was there so early but as I looked up at him from my desk I thought this must be good and replied, 'Tell them what?'

'I'm going on *Australian Survivor.*'

Wow. He was actually selected. I was speechless for the moment it took for this to register, then began hounding him for more information. But he gave me nothing. He had been given the thickest contract I had ever seen to sign. As part of the contract, he had to keep all the details confidential. He was allowed to tell immediate family and work colleagues he would be absent for up to three months or so, but nothing more.

To his credit he took the contract and confidentiality part very seriously. He didn't want anything to jeopardise this opportunity. I hadn't seen him this exhilarated for a very long time, there was suddenly plenty of pep in his step.

He was selected as one of what I understood to be eighteen people who were to be taken to the remote and rugged Whalers Way at Port Lincoln in South Australia and the location Channel Nine had chosen for filming the series. They had selected sixteen contestants, with two alternates as emergencies. Rob was initially slotted in as number seventeen, an alternate. Something then must have happened to one of the original sixteen before filming began and a spot opened. Rob was now a cast member of *Australian Survivor*.

He spent three months or so away from his life in Melbourne. I was left to try to keep Hush rolling along on my lonesome. We had no idea where he was or what was happening the whole time he was away. There was zero contact. I had to try to explain why Rob was not around to so many people over those months that I lied my arse off and I am sure there were some who thought something dastardly had happened to him.

Then one evening about three months after he had disappeared, the phone rang. 'Pete, it's Rob.'

'Hey! How are you? Where are you?' I replied.

There was silence and I thought we had lost the phone connection. But he was still there, although barely able to talk. I'd never heard his voice so weak, so emotional. 'I'm in a hotel room, we've finished. I'm not good, really struggling.'

He had spoken with his wife Dusty, and I think mum and dad before this call, so he was already teary. I told him to call me tomorrow and get some sleep as he sounded exhausted.

'Yep all right, just wanted to say I'm okay and it's all finished, should be home next week or so.' He then asked, 'How is business travelling? If it's not good, don't tell me, I won't be able to handle any bad news right now.'

I assured him all was good. Truly, it wasn't, but I saw no need to upset him right now. Before hanging up I asked, 'How did you go?'

'Can't say anything mate, chat tomorrow.'

With that he hung up. But I was left with a tiny sense he might have gone okay.

When I first caught up with Rob on his return to Melbourne, he was almost unrecognisable to the man he was before he left. He had lost 13 kg and looked so fragile and gaunt it was hard to comprehend. When I gave him a hug all I could feel was ribs. He was still an emotional wreck. I kept thinking he had better have won this thing because if he hadn't it clearly wasn't worth the emotional and physical damage he was suffering.

He told me when he first jumped into the shower at the motel following his return, the dirt was still flushing off his skin and out of his pores fifteen minutes later. He was downright filthy and stank to high heaven. Once he looked at his naked self in a mirror for the first time in months he broke down in tears. He couldn't believe how he looked. If it wasn't a full-blown mental breakdown, then it was damn close.

Over the next few months he took a lot of time to recover, be with his family and try to return to normal life. Being away from home for so long was not easy for him or his wife Dusty. Like all marriages, they had their challenges but this one was unique. Distance and uncertainty of what was happening in both their lives meant emotions were at an all-time high. It was tough going for them both.

Whalers Way in Port Lincoln was a very strange selection as a location to film this series. Nearly every *Survivor* filmed around the world is set in a tropical environment. Whalers Way was anything but tropical. It was acutely cold and wet most of the time. The conditions contestants faced were unlike anything seen before or since. It became so treacherous that Rob approached the producers (which was considered a no no…) to threaten they would all go on strike and not take any further part. The cast appointed him as their representative to speak with the producers. He told them there were real fears among the group of getting hypothermia, or even dying. My understanding is that from this point on, the contestants were provided with a little more clothing and warm rainproof jackets to help cope with the conditions. Even in the early stages of the game Rob was showing leadership within the group. Yet he knew by taking responsibility for speaking directly with the producers and crew he was risking his own chances of continuing in the game.

The exciting part for the rest of us was when Channel Nine finally began airing the series. There was no more hiding where he had been, and it was now public knowledge he was on the show. The press started to ramp up that Rob would be in the show, especially in Melbourne where he was well known through football. We were full of anticipation to see what he had been put through. I was particularly keen to see him camping or fishing. It's fair to say he wasn't exactly the outdoorsy type of bloke. In his defence, he had slept in a tent before, albeit in the backyard of home. In terms of fishing ability, well that was simply non-existent. I'm confident it would have been hard going for him to even put a worm on a hook. I couldn't wait to see him roughing it out in the bush. I'm the same by the way, so not having a go…

It was surreal to see the opening segment of the series. In the first few minutes we see a bunch of contestants all sitting on a bus driving along a remote road toward Whaler's Way. They were all blindfolded and sitting among them was Rob. Tanned, shaven and in a singlet showing off his sporty rig, the absolute complete opposite of the man who returned from Whalers Way three months later.

Immediately I was disappointed to hear the soundtrack playing. The US version has the most hauntingly powerful music, instantly recognisable as *Survivor*. This first Australian version did not. The budget for the rights to use the US version was clearly an amount Channel Nine was not prepared to pay. It probably also explains the network's choice of Whalers Way as a location instead of a more tropical environment.

The Australian version of the soundtrack was a good attempt at something similar, but was not the real thing. I must admit this put me off right from the start. I phoned Rob immediately to see what he thought, and he was gutted. It was something which always bothered him about the series, the soundtrack. When Channel Ten picked up the rights to *Survivor* many years later, it paid for the rights to use the soundtrack from the US version. This immediately lifted the look and style and felt like the original *Survivor*. Rob would have been dirty with that.

This didn't deter us from being glued to the TV week in week out, watching each episode. Being able to speak directly with Rob during and post episodes about what went on behind the scenes was a treat. But he would strictly only discuss each episode and stuck to his vow of not telling anyone what was to come. This pissed me off. As we were getting further into the series, he kept on making it through to the next stage. He was a challenge beast due to his physical strength and fitness. He was emotional and very raw at times reflecting on missing his little family, wife Dusty and young son Gabriel. This made me tear up every time.

His social game was going as well as we expected. Rob had always been someone who people gravitated towards. His sense of humour and personality made him very popular with everyone, young and old. We never had any doubts the social game would be easy for him. I was worried though how his tolerance levels would cope with being in camp so close to strangers eating loudly in front of him. Thankfully for him and his game, rice was the main staple of their diet. If crisps were on the menu in those first few days, he would have been the first voted out. No doubt.

It was hilarious to watch his facial hair growing longer by the day. Many years earlier, when Rob first started to shave, older brother Graham showed him how. He told him the whole face should be shaved, more to rile his younger brother than for any serious reason. He must have stuck to this instruction as the years went on, because as his whiskers started to sprout without shaving each day on the show, his whole face was soon covered with a beard, right up to the eyeline. His brothers thought this was one of the highlights of watching each week. He detested looking at himself on screen with the beard. But we couldn't get enough of it.

Rob being Rob, he was also getting more and more concerned about how he was coming across on the show. He would ask me, 'Was I an arsehole last night?' or 'Did that look bad?' and so on. *Survivor* is a game that demands you must tell the odd white lie, be a little conniving, burn trust. That is what it entails to make it to the end. Rob found this excruciating to watch knowing all his gameplay was right there on screen, for all to see, especially those he cared most about.

As editors ourselves, we knew there would be some creative storytelling going on behind the scenes. He was very dubious and uncertain about how he would be portrayed, or how various events would be edited together. How good or bad you appeared on screen all came down to what the show's producers decided to run as a storyline. Many times, once a show had aired, Rob would say, 'They made that part up' or 'They cut my dialogue there, left out what else I said,' which could misconstrue what he was really saying. But all in all I thought he was given a good run from the producers as some of the other contestants were portrayed far worse.

I used to tell him mum was calling me daily, weeping about how her son was such a lowlife. How did he ever turn out to be such a despicable human being? He was still rather fragile, so this didn't help his state of mind.

While the series was being aired, I was also preparing for my wedding to Ness, which was only weeks away. Rob was the best man, so this was a good distraction for him and the *Survivor* hype surrounding him. Our wedding was scheduled for ten days before the big finale show. Rob was still in the game, among the last half dozen still capable of winning. He would give us absolutely nothing by way of information as to if he was to be voted out, get to the final three, final two — anything. We just could not get him to fess up. At our wedding, the poor guy was hounded by friends and family all day long about the series as it was so close to the end.

I could sense he was nervous. Why be nervous if you know you've been voted out, I pondered. In my own mind I assumed he had at least made the top three. I would say this to him and ask for a nod, a wink, a cough, anything to tell me without telling me. He would still give me donuts.

It was time to resort to another method of dragging something out of him. I knew he wanted Ness and I to attend the big finale, which was to be filmed live at Crown Casino with Eddie McGuire hosting. The problem for us was it was scheduled during our honeymoon. I remember saying to him, 'Really sorry mate, but we won't be able to make the finale.'

'What are you talking about?' he grumpily replied.

'We're on our honeymoon, what do you expect?'

He mulled this over and begrudgingly accepted it was not a bad excuse. This is when I threw out, 'But if I knew you had at least made it to the final three maybe we would make the effort to leave the honeymoon early and come back for the night.'

He looked at me and gave me a little eyebrow lift.

'You don't need to say anything, just give me a nod if you think it might be worth it if we made the effort to leave our honeymoon early.'

He stared at me with no expression, gave a quick nod and left the room trying to convince himself that he hadn't acknowledged me at all. I knew then he was in the final three. My wedding, honeymoon and then the *Survivor* finale with Rob in contention. What a brilliant two-week period of my life.

When we entered the Crown complex we were treated like VIPs. The families and close friends of the contestants were seated in the front rows. From memory they showed the last three episodes of the series. This culminated in all the contestants seated on stage for the live reading of the final votes, and announcement of the winner.

Rob had indeed made the final three. He then made it through to the final two. We sat there in the front row as the final tribal council votes were read out. Looking at Rob on stage you could feel the enormity of the moment for him. Get the most votes and win $500,000 along with a new car. Life changing.

They love to drag it out at this point, taking their time and building the tension. It was torturous but worth the wait.

He won.

He won by a landslide.

It was one of the great moments in my life to see him win. To see the relief flow through him. We were allowed up on stage immediately to congratulate him. I hugged him tight and told him how proud I was to be his brother.

This was the one and only *Australian Survivor* to be produced by Channel Nine. Many years later Channel Ten rebooted the series. With television networks never wanting to acknowledge their competitors, Channel Ten has never made even the slightest mention of that first *Australian Survivor* series. In Channel Ten's eyes it never happened. However, it does exist online where Wikipedia, for example, provides a thorough breakdown of all contestants, the voting and challenges for all episodes.

I understand Channel Ten's thinking completely but it still irks me to this day. Every season it promotes and lauds the best players in *Australian Survivor* history. The problem is it can never be accurate until the contestants on the first series are also included. But they never will be as there are too many politics between stations.

I am clearly biased, but Rob was the best player in *Australian Survivor* history. Despite the brutal arctic conditions and extreme landscape the series was played in, he still won. Put him on any of the other subsequent tropical *Survivor* series and I know he would still have dominated.

And also obtained a super tan. He was made for it. Full stop.

CHAPTER 13

CELEBRITY

'I think you have officially graduated to D-grade celebrity status,' I told Rob at the *Survivor* finale afterparty, as people clambered over each other to speak with him and get a photo. 'That's harsh, I prefer to think it's more of a solid C,' was his response.

He was doing his best to handle all the attention flowing his way but was visibly uncomfortable. Only an hour or so before, he had learnt that five hundred thousand bucks was about to be deposited into his bank account. His head was still spinning. All he wanted to do was to go home and let it all sink in, but commitments to Channel Nine and the post-show events had to be met. I tried to help by offering him the chance to sneak out for fifteen minutes, withdraw $2k of his winnings and hit the casino floor. But that was declined.

Without much sleep and running on empty, he had to appear on Channel Nine's *Today* show very early the next morning. He looked completely wiped out and exhausted. I remember one of the hosts saying something along the lines of how shattered Rob looked for someone who had just won half a million dollars.

He was shattered, physically and emotionally, by the whole experience. But it was now over and he could start to bask in the glory of winning the title. There's no doubt he became flavour of the month in Melbourne. He was making appearances on television, speaking on radio, and having articles written about him all over the place. To be honest, it was somewhat nauseating. I would often rile him by saying I was detecting slight head wobble type behaviour.

I was joking; he couldn't have cared less about being a D-grader or trying to elevate himself to a solid C. He did feel it was all a bit over the top and used to say he was sick of hearing himself. But to his credit, he was a very good operator on television and radio and very comfortable in the limelight.

In the months following his *Survivor* win, we started to refocus on Hush Productions and getting the business moving forward again. The immediate pressures of a lack of income had been alleviated to a large degree by Rob's recent financial gain. Outside of the business we were both now in a stable financial position. He had unbelievably defied the odds of two brothers winning large purses of coin. His long-held desire to win big money had become a reality, on a reality show. His past casino visits to try to win $50 in cash were well and truly behind him.

We decided to let go of our office in Burglars Lane...and took the bold move of purchasing a share in a commercial property where we could run our business. We also started to use the moniker of Hushh. The company remained as Hush Productions, but we liked the simplicity and style of referring to ourselves as Hushh. We had some incredible people and talent starting to work with us, invest in us, and/or advise us over this period.

It is impossible to name everyone during that time, but we really started to grow and thrive when we had significant backing from a man called Simon Hammond. Simon wanted to be part of what we were doing and joined us in the Hushh venture. He was instrumental to us during those years, not only financially, but by bringing passion and a fresh exuberance to the office each day. Rob and I loved having Simon around the place.

Most of the work we were undertaking was with AFL football, the clubs and the players. With a team of freelancers, we were producing a range of content that included player highlight tapes, event openers, motivational films and various corporate short form productions. Rob's profile was already strong across the AFL landscape but when you added in the *Survivor* element, he became even more C-grade celebrity. This was hugely beneficial as it helped us procure work.

But something had changed in our personal dynamic. For the first time in my working relationship with Rob I started to feel a small separation. It was only slight, but the *Survivor* win changed something within him. We both always knew that he was the figurehead and front man for our little band called Hushh.

I was at best, the bass player. But he was now getting a great deal of attention centred on him, rather than Hushh. He would do a lot of corporate and speaking gigs as Rob Dickson, *Australian Survivor* winner. I was delighted for him, he deserved it. But I could see the tide slowly turning. He went from being reliant on what we were doing together, to having other avenues of opportunity and potential income.

I had begun to move into editing and producing short pieces myself. Rob was still the man responsible for the higher profile work but encouraged me to get my hands dirty in the edit suite. This is when I really started to creatively loosen the apron strings attached to Rob. During *The Passion to Play* production we were totally driven by his vision for the film, and I supported him in whatever he decided. That was my role, project management. I was there to support and encourage him, keep pushing him along so we could make deadlines and finish the film. Often, he would ask me to watch a segment he had put together to see what I thought. I loved doing this with him but was reticent to suggest too many opinions because I had complete faith in him.

Editing or crafting a story on my own was something I began to crave. The problem being I was convinced in my own mind I wasn't good enough to even try. With such a powerful presence right next to me in Rob, who I thought was a genius, it made it very hard to think I might also have something to contribute. What was slowly happening through this process was that I was learning, I was being moulded into his method of filmmaking style, without even realising it. I had a front row seat to see how he crafted films. Hundreds and hundreds of hours watching and learning. I like to think this was his plan, but I strongly doubt it. Hushh was known for its unique style of constructing films. Emotion and impact at the heart of our work. This was all Rob.

He was loose, no doubt about it. A structured approach is not something I would describe as Rob's process. Set hours of work? Forget about it. If it were a sunny warm day in Melbourne, he would have to get an hour or so of rays. He would say he had something on, but he never fooled me; baking in a nearby park would be where he was. He operated to his time schedules. That drove me crazy. It wasn't uncommon for him to get into such a bubble during editing that he might spend all night in the edit suite. He could only really operate when he was feeling it. If not, it was time wasted.

The daily office activities, meetings or interactions which are part of a normal day in any office had no great appeal or importance for Rob. If he could avoid a meeting he would. I am the same. Not sure why but we both had this trait in spades. It didn't help when we were both directors of the same company. We could spend hours on end with each other doing anything and everything, but when it came to a business meeting, we would both scarper. We frustrated many quality individuals who came in and tried to help us in a business sense. Through no fault of their own they would inevitably move on because we were such a nightmare to try to wrangle.

I always thought it was Rob who was the problem but when I reflect on it, I was as much to blame. We were horrendous together as business operators. I believe one of the key reasons for this mindset was our reluctance to be caught up in any confrontation or conflict. We hated being in such situations. Difficult meetings about the state of our business and finances were often best avoided. It's just the way we were.

Thankfully we had one thing going for us, we could make compelling content. When I began to create and craft pieces, Rob would always be the eye looking over it. His way was the only way I knew. He loved this. We had almost identical tastes when editing in content construction and soundtracks. As brothers we were so similar in most things so it was inevitable this would filter into the work we did. We were also emotionally connected. Similar things would make us upset, cause us to cry, laugh or even get angry. The 'feel,' which is an often-used term in creative work, was very closely aligned between the two of us. It cannot all be identical though. As I grew more confident, the work between us would differ but the Hushh feel was always recognised. This made Rob more and more comfortable in letting me take control of many more projects.

My first official documentary, if you could call it that, was *The Passion to Play — Outtakes*. Rob had given me licence to make this for a DVD release. One of the more memorable parts of the DVD is Rob hosting it. I convinced him that with his celebrity status he should front the DVD and do the voiceover where needed. I remember filming him for this and he hated every minute of it.

'Who cares about me being on it,' he would say. Or every time he stuffed up a line, 'No one cares...I look like a wanker.'

I kept pushing him along saying, 'Just shut up and do it – this needs a D-grader to give it something a little extra.'

'Well, I'm a verified C so get someone else,' he would bite back.

I'm not sure how many DVD copies of *Outtakes* were sold. Fairly certain it was not many. A masterpiece it was not. But it gave me a thrill to see something I had made myself, sitting on store shelves among other sporting DVDs. It was the beginning of feeling I was contributing in a real way creatively to our little business called Hushh.

CHAPTER 14

AFL HALL OF FAME

'Hi, I'm Gill,' said this extremely tall and skinny man as he shook hands with us after entering the front door of Hushh. Only moments earlier, Rob and I were peeking out the front window to see who this guy was coming to help us strategically, and hopefully provide we two business clowns with some direction.

It was early evening and dark outside as the most decrepit looking old ute you could imagine parked outside our office. We were like two children sneaking a look out through the blinds as it parked. Rob said, 'Can't be him…he wouldn't be driving that piece of shit.' I agreed. We looked at each other with stunned shock as this huge guy in a suit exited this very small vehicle and made his way to our front door. I'm still not sure how he fitted into it, his knees must have been around his head while driving. Acting as cool as we possibly could, like we were surprised to be answering the door, we greeted our new friend, Gillon McLachlan.

Only a week before this Rob was having dinner with his good mate Andrew Demetriou. Over dinner they were discussing our little Hushh business and Andrew was keen to know how we were faring. Rob told him it all was going okay but we didn't have any great business sense, and had no long-term plans in place. Andrew, now the CEO of the AFL, mentioned to Rob a talented young guy who had recently joined the AFL to help it with strategy.

'He's brilliant, very smart and switched on…I think he would get on famously with you guys,' said Andrew.

Rob thought why not, it couldn't hurt. As a result, Andrew arranged for Gillon to visit the Dickson brothers over the next few weeks for a chat. It was purely a favour from Andrew to Rob which enabled this to happen.

Andrew was right. Immediately we seemed to click with Gill. He knew a little bit about our work and was keen to help us where he could. We really enjoyed his company. Over the next few months, he would catch up with us in his own time, trying to help us strategically get our house in order. Through Gillon we met his brother Hamish. It was fascinating to spend time with these two brothers. Like us, they were very close and so similar in many ways. We really enjoyed the dynamic between the four of us and the times we had with them.

One thing Rob and I admired in Gill and Hamish was their drive. Learning of their pastoralist family's background in South Australia and the financial security this afforded them, it would be no surprise to see them cruise through life without much effort. But these two were fiercely independent and driven to be a success in their own right, to forge their own path. We loved this about them.

Hamish was at the time getting under way with a huge project to create an AFL Hall of Fame precinct. It was a massive undertaking. Part of the Hall of Fame required visual content and we made a pitch to try to land some of the work. With Rob's experience and talent well known throughout the AFL, he was an obvious choice. Our team at Hushh soon began working around the clock in producing content to be featured within this new Hall of Fame complex.

Some of the epic packages Rob created were stunning. It was an interactive venue where the public would be visually taken through the experience of being a player on Grand Final Day. Rob filmed all the past legendary coaches addressing the viewer via huge screens, barking their instructions and wisdom. You were then taken into the rooms for the pre-match address. We had the legend David Parkin as coach, Garry Lyon as assistant coach and me holding the magnetic board. I was without question the worst actor ever seen in screen history. We had access to the MCG on-ground during half time of one the finals games. We filmed David Parkin re-enacting a speech to his players in the huddle. I was getting abused by mates in the crowd who I didn't even know were there.

There were plenty 'Get off the ground you flog' type of comments being shouted my way. But the results of these filming days were magnificent, the results took you right there in amongst it. The crowd were rightly confused with what the hell was going on in the middle of the ground. Cameras everywhere and David Parkin and Garry Lyon looking like they were coaching…but who were they coaching? The result on screen was like nothing we had seen before, and Rob was in his element directing the entire operation. He was a pioneer in this space for AFL Football, if not the pioneer in my opinion. To be his right-hand man through all this was such an incredible ride.

Our team at Hushh were pushing themselves to the limit in coping with the massive workload. I produced most of the club packages and our offices looked like an organised, slick, fully functioning production house. This was new territory for us.

We had been introduced to ex Nike executive Ben Crowe and his business partner Glenn Lovett. They added another element to us with their guidance and support. Ben especially would go on to be an amazing friend and mentor to Rob and me over the years.

It really was a golden time for Hushh. Structure and processes were being adhered to with a decent sized staff and the place was buzzing. There were many times Rob and I would walk around the place looking at each other with a sense of, 'Is this really happening?'

Outside of 'Hushh,' Rob was still the runner for the Hawthorn Football Club. One of his great friendships at the club was with Shane Crawford. At the time Shane was arguably one of, if not the best player in the AFL. They had discussed the idea of doing a feature documentary based around Shane's life. We were steaming along at full tilt with the Hall of Fame work but suddenly this opportunity presented itself.

Shane was keen, the club was open to giving Rob access to film within the inner sanctum, and we decided to take it on. We were able to secure a broadcast deal and funding with Channel Nine. It felt like we were doing most things right as a business. We both started feeling very secure about what the future held for Hushh.

After many months and with a totally exhausted team, we finally completed the Hall of Fame project. We attended its spectacular grand opening feeling rightly proud of the part we had played. Unfortunately, this amazing project struggled to get traction with the public and within a year or so of its launch had to close its doors. We were devastated for everyone involved, especially Hamish and all those who worked so hard to make it happen.

It was no coincidence that around this time, we started to get wobbly as a business. It seemed inconceivable as only months before we were bursting at the seams with work. The crash of the Hall of Fame hit us hard, as well as many other people and companies involved in its creation. It had taken us through a period of rapid growth and sadly we now had to let people go because of the uncertainty of what lay ahead project wise. As the leaders of our business, it was heartbreaking to let good people go. We had plans to keep growing and maintain stability. Instead, we had to take this huge step backwards.

CHAPTER 15

ACCESS ALL AREAS

'Pete, you're going to be an uncle again,' Rob announced as he entered my edit suite. His face was beaming. 'Rob that is brilliant, congratulations,' I said as I gave him a little hug. Rob and Dusty already had one son, Gabriel, and now a little brother would soon arrive to be named Byron.

I had never seen anything grab Rob's attention, interest or devotion as much as his boys. He was totally besotted with his young sons and adored being a father. If he could have spent every minute of the day with them, he would have. They made him more happy and joyful than anything I had witnessed before. It was times like this, being brothers, sharing personal news and being there for each that meant the world to me. We could let go of all the issues and difficulties of the business and simply be brothers. We had started to lose this connection over the last two years when all our focus was on Hushh. It felt like we were drifting apart.

With Hushh barely spluttering along and Rob focused on the production of the Crawford documentary, we didn't have much time together. I was trying to keep up with smaller jobs coming in and left the doco to Rob and co-producer Nicole Rogers. It was a monster of a film to make. The hours of footage shot would take many months to bring together, especially as Shane also had his own camera and provided daily video diaries.

Rob was juggling more than a few balls in the air. There was still *Survivor* stuff he was doing on the side, he had far more responsibilities at home with two young sons, and he still couldn't say no to any request for him to put something together for friends. This latter trait was one that I loved about Rob. But I also hated it, especially when it got in the way of what he was supposed to be doing with Hushh. He could do whatever he wanted outside of that but when it held up what we were supposed to be making for income, it hurt the business.

Wedding videos, birthday celebration videos, special event videos, anything you can imagine Rob would be asked to do as a favour. He didn't have the ability to say no. He never wanted to let people down or be frowned upon if he declined. He loved to make people happy with his work. So, as the Crawford documentary fell further and further behind schedule, I became more and more agitated.

The business was starting to haemorrhage money and financially we were not in good shape. There was one afternoon when we had a major blow up. I went into his edit suite to see how he was travelling and noticed he was deep in a wedding video edit for one of his mates. He had been working on this for days. We were lagging behind schedule for the doco and he was spending his time on this. As in nearly all such cases it was free of charge.

I couldn't hold back any longer, this had been going on for far too long. 'What the fuck are you doing?'

'What?' he fired back.

'How can you be doing a wedding video when we need you to finish this film?'

That set him off and for the first time in my memory we were involved in a full blooded, angry, verbal stoush. It wasn't pretty. He told me to stay out of his business and without him, there wouldn't even be a Crawford doco.

I stormed out and went home. He was right, of course; without him there wouldn't even be the production with Shane. But, in my opinion, it was still wrong that he had taken his eye off the bigger picture with Hushh.

As was the case whenever we had a tiff, he or I would ring not long after to chat through it. A few hours later he called, and we talked it out. We were both emotional and understood where each other was coming from, but still finished by leaving it unresolved and simmering in the background. This summed up who we were. Non-confrontational. It was easier to let any issue slip through to the keeper. I never wanted to upset or hurt him and neither did he with me. We just pushed on.

The business was right on the edge of oblivion towards the end of the Crawford production. There were many reasons we couldn't pull it together financially. Primarily, the Crawford doco took too long to make. In this sense it was a failure. If we had managed to have some other decent paying projects locked in and running alongside it, then we might have had a better result, but we didn't. I was working on smaller video productions, but they were not high paying enough to sustain the rest of the business. This is the reality of video/film production, it is solely reliant on the ability to keep well-funded projects flowing through the door.

On the positive side, the Crawford doco *Access All Areas* was a wonderful film. Rob, Shane and Nicole had created a brilliant piece of work. Shane's honesty and raw emotion were compelling viewing. The access he provided was unprecedented. Again, Rob had created a unique and ground-breaking AFL film. Shane Crawford was and is a star. Channel Nine were thrilled and it was released to much public acclaim. If you haven't seen it, look it up. *Access all Areas, Shane Crawford Exposed*. Be prepared for a little naked action though…what would a Rob Dickson film be without some nudity involved?

CHAPTER 16

THE COLLAPSE

It had been nearly five years since we opened the doors of Hush Productions. Along the way we had been guided and advised by many outstanding people. We had financial partners who supported and believed in us. They had all spent many hours working closely with us, trying to harness this creativity into an ongoing successful entity. But in the end, we just couldn't sustain it. Rob and I had earned very little during our time in the business. Most of the investment by individuals or earnings from projects was poured into the work, not huge salaries for us. This was possible only because Rob and I had some financial security behind us thanks to our Lotto and *Survivor* wins. If not for this, we may well have had to close the doors much earlier.

There are many reasons businesses collapse and for us it was a culmination of several things. Creatively, Rob was without peer in video production. But he was not what I would term speedy in his process. He would work on something until he thought it was perfect. This was one of the reasons the end results were so brilliant. But when you don't have big budgets for certain projects, it becomes a problem when it is taking too long to complete. This was happening more and more as we went on.

I felt we were accepting every job that presented itself, regardless of how much money it was worth to us. We took them all on because we needed cash flow. Too often the hours of work required for what we were producing fell well short of the money we were being paid to create it. I was as much to blame in all these decisions as anyone.

Years earlier we had dreams of building and expanding into a large production company. But the realities of that didn't really suit either of us. We weren't financially driven nor had the business acumen and intensity required to reach and maintain that level of growth. Our individual focus had always been solely on the work. Everything else would take a back seat when we were in that bubble of crafting the best possible work of which we were capable. At the time, Hushh had an enormously popular reputation for the films it produced. Rob had built that from scratch with his talent. I firmly believe we changed the landscape of AFL and other sporting productions over that period. Hushh was innovative and unique in the work we created, but in the end it wasn't enough.

Financially the business was a bust, but we also understood that, as brothers, we needed to separate from each other for a while. We needed to do that in order to become brothers again. We had lost something between us.

'You don't trust me anymore do you,' Rob once said to me

in my edit suite as we sat reflecting on how it had come to this. I remember looking at him and not saying anything. He was visibly upset at the non-response. I wanted to say, 'Of course I do' but I was struggling and couldn't get the words out. It's ridiculous because I absolutely trusted my brother and best friend. I trusted him with my life.

But I had lost that blind trust in our working relationship that we had at the very beginning. My connection with Rob was hanging by a thread. We had stopped communicating. There was a lot going on in his life that I had no idea about. Normally he would share every minuscule detail with me, as I would with him. But we had become stuck in this daily work grind and let that side of us slip. We had lost the passion and energy which overflowed in those early days. The excitement of being with each other every day, the anticipation of what might lay ahead of us, was like a drug. Now, with all the drama engulfing the business, it was clear we were utterly sick of each other. It was time to call time on Hush Productions.

It was sad and depressing, but in many ways also a relief. It felt like a massive weight had been lifted off my shoulders. As leaders of the business, the responsibility to those who work for you is the priority. The constant fear of not being able to keep staff working or be able to remunerate them adequately is never ending. So, from this perspective it released some pressure.

But it still burned, I felt a complete failure. We had let so many people down by not making a successful go of the whole thing. People like Simon Hammond who had invested in us and believed in us, we failed him. We had terrific, talented people working with us and we couldn't guarantee them any more work. We failed them. We had so many others who contributed along the way to our baby called Hush Productions. I was so grateful to each one of them.

After we locked the doors of our offices for the last time, Rob and I went to the cafe next door for lunch. We ordered the same grilled chicken schnitzel salad rolls that we ate religiously each day. Talk about creatures of habit. I remember Rob being more emotional than I expected. He was gutted.

We were still coming to terms with the fact our little adventure together had ended. We wouldn't be seeing each other daily from now on. We reminisced, I got a bit teary which is never a surprise, and for the first time in many months we connected simply as brothers again. Even though it had ultimately failed, we thought we had at least made an impact with our films over the years with Hushh. We believed we had contributed in a major way to the AFL and sporting landscapes with our work. The fact we were not classically trained in documentary filmmaking and created our own way was something of which we were proud. It always felt like we were outliers to the real documentary making set, which suited us just fine.

As we left the cafe, I gave him a pat on the back and invited him and the family around for dinner in a few weeks' time. We hadn't done something as simple as that for so long.

'Perfect, see you then,' he said with his cheeky grin and waltzed out of the cafe for the last time, leaving me with the bill, not for the first time.

CHAPTER 17

ROB DICKSON PRODUCTIONS

'What's your plan workwise going forward?' my wife whispered as our recently born first child, Abby, slept in her arms. We hadn't really discussed at length what was next for me following the Hushh collapse. I had decided to take a solid break and spent a few months at home really enjoying being a new dad. Obviously, this couldn't go on indefinitely and I had to start earning some money again. This was daunting for me to even think about. My security blanket of Rob was gone.

Rob had slowly begun returning to video production work under his own steam. He had called his new entity Rob Dickson Productions. When he first told me what he was calling it I laughed.

'What are you laughing at?' he enquired.

'It's just funny, that's all. Hush Productions was essentially Rob Dickson Productions anyway so maybe you've finally got the name right.'

He rolled his eyes and tried to claim that was bullshit but we both knew it to be true.

For someone who had grown up without swearing at any stage, Rob had slowly become quite the potty mouth.

'No need for the language old boy,' I would often poke him with.

'You can talk,' he would counter.

Fair point, I wasn't what you would call a swearing machine, but I gave it a good go when in the mood. But for Rob this was a significant shift over the years from how he behaved while growing up. There is no doubt that once he arrived at the Hawthorn Football Club his outlook and attitude towards life began to change. To me it felt like once he was released from the tight grip mum had held on to him at home, he started to explore more of what life had to offer. What better way to get a real-life education into sex, drugs and rock 'n' roll than become an AFL player? That's probably a tad harsh and unfair slant on it, but it was the 1980s after all.

Because of his strong faith and beliefs he battled morally at times with the rights and wrongs of his approach to life. Out of all the Dickson boys he was the cleanskin of the bunch. By no means was this a bad thing. If anything, he had the fortitude to live and stick to his beliefs, which I respected no end. But I certainly began to see subtle differences in him once he reached his mid-twenties. He would begin to throw the odd swear word into conversation. Girlfriends might stay over, which never used to happen. The lengths he would go to in order to hide any evidence of such dalliances if mum was visiting were extraordinary. Any proof of a girl's presence in the house would be hidden well before mum entered. His fear that she might find out he was up to some non-Christian like behaviour was too much for him to contemplate. He was very, very popular with the ladies, so in my mind it was inevitable that he would crack at some point. Everyone I knew, including me, battled our hearts out trying to impress the fairer sex. For Rob, it was effortless; they were always drawn to him. But there came a time when all this pretending with mum came to a screaming halt.

He had taken a weekend trip to Morwell to visit her during his Hawthorn days. I vividly remember him walking in the front door of our Melbourne house on Sunday evening, with the most mortified look on his face I had ever seen. Hours earlier in Morwell, he had gone for his regular jog. Upon his return from the run, he walked into the house to see mum sitting at a table crying. He was initially shocked to see her crying but not as shocked as he was seconds later when he observed what she was crying about. Laid out on the table right in front of her were dozens of naked pictures of Rob and a girl he was seeing at the time. During his jog, mum had grabbed his car keys and opened his locked car, then proceeded to unlock the glove box. There she found an envelope full of photos.

If this sounds like a horrendous invasion of privacy, that's because it is a horrendous invasion of privacy. But this was our mum. She was a snoop of the highest order. Rob thus endured the biggest grilling and interrogation he had ever received from his mother. This was a grown man, living his own adult life, with his mother hysterically berating him about being a sinner and a disgrace.

I genuinely tried to empathise with him as he was explaining what happened, but it was hard when I was physically bursting, and rolling around the floor in uncontrollable laughter.

'Well, looks like I'm now the number one son, you had a good run though' I spluttered out.

'You're welcome to it,' he screamed back.

For anyone other than Rob this story might be slightly humorous. Apparently even the girl featured thought it was hilarious. But, for Rob, it was far from funny. It was totally unacceptable, and it changed everything in his relationship with mum. She realised he wasn't the perfect son according to her expectations. And he felt she had overstepped a line and was completely out of order.

He finished off his rant on the Sunday evening by yelling, 'Compared to everyone else I know and what they get up to I am a bloody saint, but mum now thinks I actually might be the Antichrist!'

I couldn't resist one final crack. 'You're no saint, mate, you just swore then...bloody...'

He skulked off up the hallway shaking his head. I couldn't look at him for about a week without chuckling. He was right though. I lived with him and witnessed how he approached life, and treated people firsthand. By no means was he perfect, but he was far closer to saintly compared to most others I knew, by a long way.

Rob was someone I would describe as emotionally intelligent.

This emotional intelligence was very evident in his filmmaking. He had an incredible natural way of storytelling which touched the soul. It made you feel something. Our upbringing and life experiences, including those moments with our mum were integral to our make-up. We were the sum of all those parts and, for better or worse, we were emotional beings.

He would always tell me that whatever I produced and crafted in film, it needed to make an impact, make those watching feel something, get them thinking. If you didn't achieve this, then it was not working. Whenever I was in doubt whether something reached that level or not, Rob was only metres away to give me his opinion. This was invaluable. But from now on I would have to trust my own instincts, there was only me. Was I capable or merely a poor man's Rob Dickson trying to make a living?

These were the thoughts consuming me as I spoke with Ness about the future. 'I'm going to try to keep progressing and hopefully pick up work. I've learnt from Rob, developed skills, and feel like I'm okay at what I do. Let's see what happens.'

Ness was supportive and encouraged me to go out on my own and give it a go. I spoke with Rob and told him I was naming my new little company Hushh Vision. He liked that. 'Very visionary,' he quipped. It also kept a tiny connection with what we had both created years earlier. I told him I was not nearly bold enough to go with Peter Dickson Productions, which would have come across as something more akin to... Who?... Productions.

CHAPTER 18

ESSENCE OF THE GAME

'No offence mate but this place has a fair stench to it.' It was some months later and I had entered the new Hawthorn based office of Rob Dickson Productions and was compelled to say something. 'You kind of get used to it,' was Rob's response. His new working abode was directly above an Indian restaurant. It was without heating or cooling and had a rich musty odour to it. Throw in the afternoon wafts of curry and it was quite the experience for the nostrils. We were checking out each other's new offices, Rob had been to my digs in South Melbourne and now I was over at his in Hawthorn.

He was trying to install some kind of dodgy air-conditioning unit in his edit suite. I immediately understood why. Within twenty seconds of walking up the stairs into the place I was sweating bricks. It was steaming hot in there, add the smells of the delicious Indian curries being cooked below, and you would have been forgiven for thinking you were in Mumbai in mid-summer.

'Can you help me with this?' He was gesturing for me to assist him install a mobile air-conditioning unit's air valve or pump, not even sure what it was. It needed to be put through the open window to allow ventilation or something along those lines according to Rob. We were appalling handymen, so this was a real task. We managed to get it working but the main problem was his window wouldn't be able to be locked. It would be permanently open with this monstrosity of a tube hanging out on the sill.

'Not a problem…it's all good, it will be fine,' he said. For a moment I was about to grill him about it not being fine with his window backing on to a laneway and car park which could easily be accessed by the thieving fraternity. But then I realised I no longer worked in the office with him. No need to say anything, his problem now. Thankfully, he cranked up his new mobile air-conditioner and the place started to cool down, marginally.

As we sat there chatting, he was telling me about his new project. It was a big documentary feature called *The Essence of the Game*. It had evolved from an idea Rob had during the making of one of his AFL season launch films. The AFL had begun to contract Rob to make a short film each year about the story of the previous season's Grand Final. It became a regular addition to the AFL's annual season launch. I remember thinking, 'Wow, he's already locked in a major doco.'

He was also producing various other smaller productions but nothing on the scale of what this would be. I was travelling okay with regular projects across some AFL clubs and racing, as well as some cricket work, but didn't have anything of this magnitude on the radar. I was delighted for him. To see him slowly getting back into the swing of making films again after all the dramas with Hushh was really pleasing. It was in his wheelhouse and he was more than capable taking this on himself. I was nowhere near ready to tackle something of this size alone back then, not even close to ready.

The AFL and Channel Seven had agreed to back him so he was off and running with production. He had assembled a small team of freelancers and was excited about getting back into the making of another feature. He asked me if there was any part of this project that I might be interested in helping him with. I'm certain it was a question more out of courtesy than anything else. We were both enjoying our own spaces and time away from work issues together and I wasn't keen to jump back into all of that yet. He was feeling the same way, I'm sure. I remember telling him this was his baby. I would carry on with my own thing for a while. Just being a brother without all that hanging over us was also something I was revelling in again.

Back on the home front Ness had raised the possibility of us going overseas for six to twelve months. She had been given an opportunity to work in Cork, Ireland, in obstetrics. We had added another addition to our little family with beautiful Sasha, a sister for Abby. It was perfect timing for us to make the move. Work was steady for me but by no means overflowing. I had no responsibilities to anyone else in a working sense, only me. I really liked that. It gave me a sense of calm that whatever decision I made, the only effect it would have would be on me. If we were ever going to take a trip like this, it was now.

Ness was keen and determined to experience working in Ireland, so off we went. Flying all the way across the world with our two toddlers in tow. A year of being a stay-at-home dad was now my main occupation.

During our time in Cork, I had very little contact with Rob. The odd email or telephone call checking in with how he was going was about the extent of it. But it was patently obvious he was stressed and fully overwhelmed with the workload he was buried in while making this film. He knew this was his project of a lifetime, everything he had achieved to date in his filmmaking career was leading to this. It added even more pressure in his own mind knowing it had to be his masterpiece of masterpieces.

When we returned from our Ireland jaunt in late 2008, I had to focus on establishing my business again and start picking up some work. The office I had previously operated from was no longer available, so I needed a new workspace. Within a couple of days of being back in Melbourne, I went to see Rob. I had missed him more than I expected while away and was excited to see him.

I wandered up the stairs of his office and smiled at the familiar musty curry scent of the building. He was in his edit suite surrounded by hard drives, pages of notes and generally looking dishevelled and very tired. We hugged and it was so good to see him again after so long. We went out for a coffee or, in his case, a hot chocolate. That was his drink of choice, he hated coffee. You could always detect a slight eyebrow raise from those taking the order, really a hot chocolate? What are you ten? That's what I envisaged they were thinking each time he ordered one. He couldn't have given two hoots about what they thought though, he loved his hot chocolate.

Rob was keen to hear about the trip and wanted to know what I was going to do now. I mentioned I was looking for some office space and without hesitation he said, 'Use the empty office where I am.'

It was not something I had expected. After all we had been through in the last few years, the thought of again sharing office space hadn't entered my mind. The break had worked wonders for us and our relationship. Knowing we had our own separate little entities meant the challenges we had before were no longer the same. I took him up on the offer and was soon in residence in an office directly above the Indian restaurant.

It was a very weird few months that followed. Weird in a sense that I was scratching away with some of my own smaller projects without too much pressure or stress hanging over me. But twenty metres away I could see Rob in his edit suite sinking under the huge weight of responsibility he had on his shoulders to deliver this film to Channel Seven. I almost felt guilty in a way, but this was his baby and I was reluctant to poke my nose into his business. If he asked for an opinion or some help, of course I provided it, but I was more of a sounding board on which he could vent his frustrations rather than having any real involvement in the film. He had some wonderful assistance from a small team including Galia and Alan Hardy, Holly Salisbury, Greg Blakely, Justin Powell, Lincoln Cleak and others. He was in good hands. Most of his team would continue to do amazing work and be of enormous help to me with my own films in the future.

Rob was really battling as he got closer and closer to delivery deadlines. He had provided a rough-cut draft to Channel Seven. This is the point where a filmmaker's stress levels go into overdrive. You question everything. Is it any good? Will they like it? What could I have done better? This internal interrogation relentlessly floods your thoughts. So, when he received the feedback from a Channel Seven executive about changes that needed to be made with the film before they would accept it, Rob flipped his lid. He burst into my tiny edit suite with a page full of notes and changes required. He was livid.

'Take a look at all this shit!' He was shaking with anger.

The changes they demanded were not insignificant. It would mean reshaping the film into something Rob was dead against. As the filmmaker you live the process 24/7, you have done nothing but let it consume your being since you started filming. When an outsider suddenly enters the frame and gives their take on your work it can incense you.

'That bloke, he has no idea.' Rob was now full steam. 'I'm not changing a single thing; they can all get stuffed.'

I looked over the page of notes and was soon as angry as Rob, and it wasn't even my project. He had me just as riled up.

'What are you going to do?' I gingerly asked.

'I don't know, I'm so over the whole thing.'

He sounded defeated. I felt disappointed for him. He thought he'd reached the finish line but this demanded so much more work. Work he didn't agree with, and thought would ruin the feel of the whole film.

This was new territory for Rob. Previously he was always in a position where he had total creative control of the films he made, there was very little or no recourse. What he made was what was released. But this was a different beast. The network had contractual rights to demand changes it felt were required. Rightly or wrongly, it has its own take on what makes good television. Specifically, what makes good television for Channel Seven, and often that decision is in the hands of a single person. When the commissioning is from the network, you have no choice but to fall into line. It sucks big time if you think its opinion is shit.

More than anything else, I could see the self-doubt and deflated confidence consuming Rob. It was crushing to him to think his masterpiece was viewed as flawed by a network executive. These emotions are inherent in our make-up. The sense of failure is taken to heart and deeply affects how we view ourselves. We beat ourselves up emotionally over and over and struggle to let it go. Unfortunately, that is who we are. I felt everything he was going through, I knew what it was doing to him, and yet was powerless to help.

Begrudgingly, and without any enthusiasm or acknowledgement that the views of the network were correct, he tweaked and reshaped as much, or as little more like it… as he could before official sign-off. His producer, Galia Hardy, had worked tirelessly to appease Channel Seven and was a wonderful help to Rob in convincing and cajoling them to tone down many of the requested changes. One change requested was for a voiceover which the network scripted themselves. This was something Rob was dead set against. But he had to concede something.

Collingwood great Nathan Buckley, who was working with the network at the time, was offered up to be the voice. Rob and Nathan were good mates, so Rob agreed. Thankfully during the recording of the voiceover, Nathan thought much of the script was pointless and decided to only use portions of it. This pleased Rob no end. He felt vindicated that someone of Nathan's pedigree in the game had agreed a lot of the voiceover requested was completely unnecessary.

Exhausted and not entirely satisfied with the end product because of the network's interference, he finally completed and delivered *The Essence of the Game* documentary. I thought it was magnificent. I was happy for Rob, he had poured his heart and soul into his vision for the film, and it showed. To this day it is still talked about as one of the best football documentaries made in this country. Now it was time for Rob to take a well-deserved extended break.

One aspect of documentary filmmaking for Rob and I is once we have completed a film, it takes us a long time to recharge. We need to let it go mentally and to refresh before thinking of taking on anything further. Again, it's that emotional connection we pour into the craft that eventually wears you down, it's unavoidable.

In the months following the release of *The Essence of the Game*, Rob and his family began planning a trip to South Africa for a much-needed holiday. I hadn't seen him much in the office as it was the last place he wanted to be for a while. But before his trip to South Africa he came in to discuss the potential for us to move out of the 'Mumbai building' when he returned from South Africa.

'I think I can strike a deal for us to move into the Glenferrie football oval offices,' he said, very chuffed with himself.

I was a little surprised and said, 'The actual offices underneath the grandstand?'

'Yep! Let's go for a walk right now and check them out.'

Five minutes later, Rob, his bookkeeper Holly Salisbury and I took a stroll up Glenferrie Road and into the bowels of the old Glenferrie Road football oval grandstand. Hawthorn football club had long since departed the ground and were now based in Waverley. The old club offices underneath were up for lease. This was the era of controversial former State Premier Jeff Kennett's presidency of the club. As Rob took us through these offices he claimed the old office and boardroom of Jeff Kennett as the spaces he would take. He had his feet up on the boardroom table and put on the worst Jeff Kennett impersonation imaginable.

It was exciting for him. His old hunting ground, the place he loved and where he had spent so many years would again be home for him. It wasn't exactly in great nick. It was rundown and the totally abandoned look was somewhat depressing, but that didn't bother Rob. I thought why not, plenty of space and there was air-conditioning — and not a whiff of curry in the air, only the barest scent of liniment and old footy boots prevailed.

We agreed that on his return from South Africa this would be our new digs. It was the best feeling between us in years, we had thoughts and chats about working together on some future projects. I was happy.

On the way back from the Glenferrie inspection, I stopped off to get some groceries and Rob came into the supermarket with me. He was talking excitedly about his trip to South Africa. He was leaving in the next few days. I got to the counter with my trolley and noticed Rob was looking a little suspicious. As the contents of my trolley were laid out at the pay register, there was a huge box of condoms front and centre. The checkout person gave me a little look of embarrassment. One of Rob's favourite pastimes was to publicly embarrass me. Whenever we shopped there would always be one item in among my purchases that I hadn't put there. Could be lady's panties, stockings, condoms, creams for all sorts of ailments, anything that would stand out among the groceries. I should have known better, but it had been a long time since we had been in a supermarket together. As I stood there with a very red face trying to convince the checkout person the condoms were not in fact mine, all I could hear was Rob chortling a few feet away. All I said to him was, 'Well played.'

After we returned to the office, it was time to say farewell and wish him all the best for his holiday. I remember asking him if he was going to try his foolproof method of gaining an upgrade on the plane. In his mind it was foolproof because it had worked before. As the cabin staff rattled past with the trolley, he would deliberately bump the back of it and act like the trolley had run over his finger. He had a very dodgy out of shape finger gained through an old football injury. As soon as the steward saw his finger, they were convinced the trolley had caused it to be bent out of shape. With Rob acting like he was in serious pain, he would be offered apology after apology and eventually an upgrade to business class to help ease his distress. This had actually worked. But Rob assured me he wouldn't be attempting it this time as his family were also on board and it would be a bit out of order.

I remember saying, 'Have fun mate, safe travels.'

They would be the last words I ever spoke to him.

Dad in 1960, posing in his Australian baseball kit. A big hitting centre fielder

Beach baby: mum and Rob at the beach

Rob the cute baby and already looking tanned

An early connection: the author clutching on to Rob, with Don, Graham and Sue behind

I look enthralled as mum reads me the twenty-third psalm.

Paper boy: Rob heads off on his Heathmont round

Now we are six: Ricky arrives to complete the six Dickson brood

DIY skills on display: Rob renovating our three-story treehouse

Safety at play: Graham, Rob in Magpies jumper and Don ensuring I don't fall fifteen-feet off the treehouse roof

*The sickly kid
skateboarding down
the family's Heathmont
driveway*

The good looking rooster

HAWTHORN FOOTBALL CLUB LIMITED
P.O. Box 32 Hawthor Vic. 3122

HAWTHORN
FOOTBALL CLUB

OF THE 80'S

Peter Dickson
50 Hazelwood Rd,
Morwell, 3840.

*Treasured mail
arrives from the
Hawthorn Football
Club*

HAWTHORN FOOTBALL CLUB LIMITE

THE NEW FORCE OF THE EIGHTIES

Correspondence to be addressed to:

The Chief Executive
P.O. Box 52
Hawthorn Vic. 3122
Telephone 819 2199

October 18, 1984

Dear Player,

On behalf of the Hawthorn Football Club I would like to extend to you an invitation to train with the Junior Reserves (Under 19's) for Season 1985.

Because of the distance from our country zone to Glenferrie Oval, three training groups will operate until the Christmas break and we have circle the training venue, we believe, is the best situated for you to attend.

1. Glenferrie Oval - Linda Crescent, Hawthorn. Commencing on Wednesday November 7, at 5.30pm and continuing every Monday and Wednesday evening until Christmas. The coach at this venue will be Mr. Ray Biffin (Junior Reserves coach).

2. Warragul Soccer Ground - Bourke Street, Warragul. Commencing on Wednesday, November 7, at 5.30pm and continuing every Monday and Wedne evening until Christmas. The coach at this venue will be Mr. Frank De (Country Development Officer).

3. Hallam - Hallam Recreation Reserve, Frawley Road, Hallam. Commer on Wednesday, November 7, at 5.30pm and continuing every Monday and Wednesday evening until Christmas. The coach at this venue will be Mr. Peter Snooks (Fitness advisor Junior Reserves).

The letter inviting me to train with Hawthorn in 1984

Still a rooster: school captain Rob in Year 10

Flying high: Seventeen-year-old Rob as a helicopter pilot with the NSCA

Rob's first job: as a cadet with the NSCA

Leaping to it: Rob in action for Morwell Tigers Football Club.

Brothers shedding shirts for no apparent reason

BACK: A Gowers, R Jencke, S Maginness, C Mew, J Dunstall, G Madigan, C Langford, S Lawrence, L Bingham, S Ralphsmith, D Brereton, J Kennedy.
MIDDLE: P Dear, R Loveridge, A Collins, D Pritchard, M Bourke, J Morrissey, G Dear, D Anderson, A Condon, C Wittman, A Demetriou.
FRONT: G Buckenara, P Curran, J Platten, G Ayres (v-capt), A Jeans (coach), M Tuck (capt), D Meagher (asst. coach), R DiPierdomenico, R Dickson, P Schwab.

Team player: Rob, front row second from right,
with his Hawthorn teammates

Running laps: Rob (and that mullet) training at Hawthorn

You're on camera: Rob filming behind the scenes at Hawthorn

Game time with Rob's great mate, Peter Schwab, in background

Favourite accessory: Rob with his Super 8 camera

Surf's up: with brother Graham on one of our many surfing trips

Two roosters, same hair: Rob and cousin Mal during house-sharing days

Rob on a promotional shoot during his Hawthorn days

*One of my
favourite pictures
with Rob:
me typically
sunburnt
and him so
annoyingly
brown*

*Champions: Rob,
on left, celebrating
Brisbane Bears
Reserves 1991 Grand
Final win*

Jubilant Bears celebrate historic victory

There are no prizes for guessing who won the AFL reserve grade grand final — jubilant Brisbane Bears players (led by, from left, Robert Dickson, Corey Bell and Steve McLuckie) are caught in full celebratory cry after their historic victory

Jackpot: Ness holding the Tattersalls million dollar cheque

Ricky, Rob and the author in Zimbabwe on Rob's wedding day

Leap of faith: me at Victoria Falls launching into what was the world's highest bungee jump

Ball's eye view: Rob with his dodgy footy-cam contraption that surprisingly worked

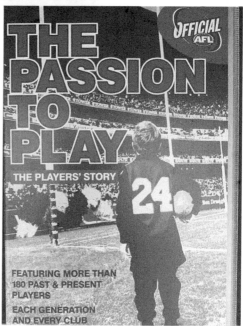

*The Passion to Play
VHS/DVD sleeve*

Best man Rob standing by my side on my wedding day

With my beautiful wife Ness and our wedding party

Funny guy: Rob thinking he's Jerry Seinfeld during his best man speech

Ness laughing a little too hard at the best man speech

CHAPTER 19

THE CALL

'I bet the front door is open anyway,' I said to Ness as we walked up the front porch steps of Rob's house. It was Easter 2009. Rob and his family were now in South Africa on their holiday. Before he'd left, I'd asked him if we could stay at his place over Easter while they were gone. We were living in Point Lonsdale and I was commuting back and forth to Melbourne for work. We wanted to spend Easter in Melbourne, so Rob had given me his house keys. I was pleasantly surprised to see the front door locked, very unlike Rob. Our two little girls were excited to see the toys and other belongings of Gabriel and Byron's on the front porch. Once we entered they were soon close to having tantrums when they realised their cousins were away on holidays.

It was a strange feeling being in the house without them, but we made ourselves at home. The girls were easy to put to bed as they were sleeping in the boys' room, which was quite a thrill for them. Ness and I were putting our bags in Rob and Dusty's room when I was taken aback by seeing a book, *The God Delusion*, on Rob's bedside table. I indicated the book to Ness and she responded with a look of surprise. It is a book I would never in my wildest dreams have imagined Rob reading. *The God Delusion* contends that a God almost certainly doesn't exist. It shocked me to see it there. I felt disappointed but had no idea why. It was Rob's personal business so why was I so intrigued by its presence?

I couldn't stop looking at it or thinking about it during the night. It made me feel as if Rob was still exploring the belief system and faith that he grew up so attached to. For some reason it made me kind of sad to know this might still be a battle for him. I decided I would discuss the book with him on his return and see what he thought of it all, knowing full well I probably would get a 'Mind your own business' in response.

On Saturday morning Ness left the house early for some exercise and took off on a bike ride. I was sitting in the kitchen and the girls were watching a cartoon show on the television. My mobile phone started to ring and I was surprised to see it was my dad calling. I thought, 'Geesh, dad's up and about early.'

'Hi dad ...' Seconds went by without any response ... and then, 'Peter ... Robert is dead.'

When I first heard his words all I could think was how blunt he was being in saying such a thing. It was as if my brain had already gone into protective mode, trying to shield me from the reality of what he was saying. Urging me to concentrate on how blunt dad was being, as if that would work.

'What...what did you just say?' The words came tumbling out of my mouth.

'Robert is dead...he died in a car crash in South Africa.'

Having to make this call and subsequent calls to all his children must have been horrendous for dad. His way, the only way he knew, was to be upfront and come straight out with the words. No pussy-footing around. He was in shock, but he accepted the responsibility to call all his kids with the news.

The call didn't last very long. Dad still had to keep contacting everyone else but assured me he would ring back shortly with further details. He had already hung up but I still had the phone to my ear saying, 'No, no, no, no' for I don't know how long.

I didn't cry immediately. It was too much to take in. Couldn't be true, there'd been a mistake, he might only be injured, all these and similar hopeful thoughts sped through my brain. I sat there in a numb and surreal fog of stunned silence. Only ten feet away directly in front of me my girls were giggling and enjoying cartoons, happy as could be. Ness had only recently left on her bike ride and would not be back for a while.

What do I do now? I had never experienced this level of shock and it swallowed me up. I tried to hide from the girls by going into the back sunroom behind the kitchen. It was hard even to walk. Here we were in Rob's house for God's sake. His very home. It was not right. Nothing was right.

Dad called back not long after. By then I had started crying uncontrollably. He explained he had received a brief call from South Africa, and it was hard to hear all the details. But Rob, Dusty, the two boys and their cousin from Zimbabwe had been in a car accident outside Sun City. Rob and Byron were dead. Dusty and their cousin had survived. Gabriel was alive but unresponsive and in hospital being monitored around the clock.

It felt like being struck by a tsunami of information and unable to comprehend any of it. I remember mum then called me. All she said was, 'Oh, Pete ...I'm so sorry.'

I couldn't believe my beautiful mum was telling me she was sorry. She had just lost her son and a grandson and here she was, trying to comfort me. I will never forget her gentle way on the phone with me. I remember letting out guttural groans, not a pleasant sound but I couldn't control it.

Then I noticed my two baby girls standing in front of me stunned, obviously with no idea what was going on and looking really scared. Abby started crying because I was crying. Thankfully, at that moment Ness walked in the front door. When she noticed me, she sprinted over to see what was wrong. All I could say was, 'Rob and Byron are dead.'

The next few hours were mainly spent speaking on the phone with my family. It was harrowing but comforting to hear all their voices. There was so much pain, with everyone feeling it equally. My phone had started relentlessly beeping with messages. I kept thinking how anyone could possibly know yet. Somehow the press had got hold of it in Melbourne. News reports from South Africa had been picked up here. There were messages from journalists on the phone asking if I was willing to chat. I mean really. No. Just no.

I walked out to Rob's backyard and fell into the foetal position on his outdoor lounge. I was trying to process everything. It was there and then I decided I had to go to South Africa immediately. I wanted to bring them home. I spoke with dad and told him I had to get on a plane as soon as possible. I was manic about it. Dad told me he was going as well and Don was also on his way to Melbourne from Gippsland, planning to come with us.

It was not long after this when I received a call from Andrew Demetriou, CEO of the AFL. I could hardly speak but I remember he was devastated. He told me the AFL would help arrange everything we needed. Apparently Rob was also on a semi-working trip for the AFL while in South Africa. He was to spend time filming with an AFL junior squad that was touring South Africa. Andrew arranged for Brian Walsh from the AFL to be our contact and sort anything we needed. When I look back now, the AFL was simply immense for our family. I'm not sure what we would have done without it cranking into action immediately. Such an emotionally draining and difficult job for anyone to have to undertake, but Brian Walsh did an incredible job.

Don arrived at Rob's house and was in a mild panic because he had issues with his passport, or rather a lack of passport with his current one no longer valid. With the help of the Australian High Commission and AFL he was able to have it fast tracked. By 10 pm he was in the city collecting his updated passport and within twenty-four hours the AFL had sorted flights for the three of us. They were on hand at any time of the day and willing to help us in any way they could. Just immense.

We had some of our extended family visit us at Rob's house during the day. It was all an immense blur. My gorgeous cousins,

Suzie and Fiona, and my Auntie Janice didn't live far from Rob and were there doing everything they could. They were grieving just as deeply, they loved Rob and he loved them. They took control of looking after our girls while everything was swirling around us. I sat on Rob's living room couch that evening trying to come to terms with the reality of what had occurred. Only hours earlier the world was a completely different place. Life was good, and I was content. Now it had flipped on its axis. It felt like any joy I had inside was completely sucked out. It was hauntingly quiet in the house now. Any step you took there was a reminder of Rob and his family. Shoes, toys, clothes, everything was a reminder. You could almost smell them.

I turned on the television as some kind of distraction. The footy was on. It felt for a millisecond that life was still normal, nothing else had stopped out there. Life went on. But during halftime the commentary team mentioned Rob and his death. That was it for me, I lost it again. It was a brutal night. As I tried unsuccessfully to get some sleep, I stared at the book on his bedside table, *The God Delusion*. All I could think was whatever Rob's views or beliefs were in his final moments, he would now know for certain whether there was a God or not.

Very early on the Sunday morning Ness drove Don and I to the airport. Dad arrived, that was tough. He was broken. I could see the aching in his face, no father should ever have to go through this. He was physically shaking. Saying goodbye at the gates to Ness was incredibly difficult. We were soon seated on the plane where I tried my utmost to sleep and stop the tears. But I didn't achieve either for the whole flight.

CHAPTER 20

SOUTH AFRICA

Looking out through the window as we descended into
Johannesburg, all I was thinking was how much I now hated
the place. I had visited South Africa some years previously for
a holiday and absolutely treasured my time there. But now I
detested the entire country. This land had taken something
from me. I vowed that once all this was over I would never
return.

Kevin Sheehan from the AFL greeted us at the airport. He
was already in the country looking after the junior squad. Such
a difficult moment for Kevin with three heavily grieving family
members, but he was magnificent. The AFL had arranged for
us to be collected at the airport and driven directly to Pretoria
Hospital. This was where Dusty, Gabriel and his cousin Glynne
had been taken. We felt embraced by the AFL, it was doing
everything it could to make our trip as comfortable as humanly
possible. It made an impossible situation that little bit easier.

The Department of Foreign Affairs had updated dad with further details on the accident. Rob had been driving and was attempting a U-turn when hit by another car. They were near Sun City. They were flown by emergency services helicopter to Pretoria Hospital.

After we had exited Customs, we were taken in a minivan directly to the hospital. With no sleep for the last forty-eight hours, I was battling and not in great shape. Dusty's brother-in-law, Gavin, met us at the entrance to the hospital where we tearfully embraced each other. I had met him several times previously and enjoyed his company. This big strong Zimbabwean man was shattered, but his son Glynne had survived the crash so he was coping with a mix of pain at the loss of Rob and Byron and relief his son had survived. Gabriel was on life support in the hospital.

When we arrived, Dusty was at Gabriel's bedside with her sister Deb and mother. My heart was breaking into pieces seeing Dusty. I gave her a little hug and kissed her hair. She was not really responding. It looked as if the shock of what was going on had put her into another place mentally. To see us arrive must have added another layer of, 'What the hell is going on here?' This was a wife and mother who had just lost her husband and son and had her other boy on life support. It was unimaginable what she was going through. In a sense it felt that we were intruding.

We had accommodation organised by the AFL at a little place within walking distance from the hospital. It wasn't recommended to walk there at night as crime was through the roof, so we had a driver take us back and forth if it was dark. Even during the day, it felt unsafe walking outside the gates. Carjacking seemed to be an hourly occurrence. Feeling as if we were in the wild west caused me to hate the place even more.

For the next few days, we spent as much time as we could sitting with Gabriel. It was the only place I really wanted to be, sitting at his bed holding his hand and talking to him about anything and everything, hoping he was listening and by some miracle, would wake up.

My brother Don was enormous support for me while in South Africa. I could lean on him, confide in him, cry, be angry, just be me. Don is far more sensible and less emotional than me. He, like Rob, knew me all too well. He knew when to leave me alone, when to calm me down and when to put his arm around me. I've always loved Don, as I do all my brothers, but this experience put him on a different level. He was mighty. I hope in some form I provided the same to him.

Dad was frantic. He went into business organisational mode. He had a funeral to arrange, he had to deal with all the official duties that accompany this kind of tragedy in another country. The Department of Foreign Affairs worked alongside him and helped with everything they could. I was happy to see him dive into all this and be occupied, it helped him escape into his own bubble. He hardly left his room as he had so much to plan and resolve. He would spend the next two years of his life sorting out all Rob's personal affairs before finally getting everything in order.

We kept holding on to the barest thread of hope that Gabriel would pull through. But his injury was too severe and the harrowing decision was made to turn off his life support. The single worst moment I've had in my life was being at his bedside when this time came. I am forever grateful I got to see Gabe, hold his hand, and sit with him for those final days. He looked like an angel. I hold that image of him in my heart to this day. I took some comfort in thinking he might now be back with his brother and dad.

Don and I then had to travel to a place I can only describe as hell on earth. It was a filthy looking town with the morgue where Rob and Byron had been taken. We had to officially identify the bodies. The guy in the office treated us with disdain. I blazed with anger towards him for his distinct lack of compassion. Don tried to calm me down saying how it was a task this bloke must have to undertake each day. There was so much death and tragedy in the area, he looked as if he was almost immune to the process. You would have to be.

The man gave me Rob's ring as part of the personal belongings returned to us. It still had blood on it. That tore me to shreds. I spent a long time cleaning that ring, over and over and over. After a seven-hour wait we were finally taken to an area where we could view the bodies. Afterwards, as we walked away, I felt I was going to be sick. No one should have to do what we had been required to do, no one. But it was our responsibility, and we did what had to be done.

I will never forget Don stopping me in my tracks and saying, 'Pete, we will never talk about what we saw to anyone, let's just keep it between us.' He grabbed me around the shoulders, almost demanding me to agree. I said, 'Of course.' So, I'm not talking about it. After a long drive back in a state of agony and numbness, we spent some time with Dusty. I gave her Rob's ring.

A small funeral was held a few days later. The plan was to have a larger memorial service back in Melbourne upon our return. It was a tiny church and I can hardly remember any of it. It was basically dad and Don, Dusty, and her family. I have some footage of it somewhere which I still cannot bear to look at.

Former West Coast Eagles captain and Gold Coast Suns coach Guy McKenna was there as part of a small AFL delegation. He took my camera and filmed some vision for us. I hope one day I will have the nerve to look through it.

Following the funeral, I was sitting with dad in his room when he broke down sobbing. It was almost like his mind and body had finally given up after all his frantic organising activity. I had never seen him this way before. He was a mess. Everything flooded over him and I was relieved to see him let it all out. He had lost his son, his favourite son and most probably his favourite person in life. He had lost his grandkids who he adored.

I had seen dad mellow since those early years when we were younger. He was amazing with the grandkids. They all loved him, and he loved to have them stay with him whenever possible for holidays. He couldn't get enough of Gabriel and Byron. When he said something about the Dickson bloodline now being lost I thought, what's he talking about?

But he kept repeating it; the Dickson surname was now lost for future generations. Graham had two girls, Don had two girls, I had two girls and Ricky had two girls. Although Sue had four boys, the difference in dad's mind was that those four boys had their dad's surname, Leak. It was old school thinking but dad is old school.

Rob was the only boy in our family who had sons. He always loved to poke me with, 'I'm the only real man amongst all the brothers as I can produce sons' as he punched his chest like Tarzan. Seeing dad losing it in his room caused me to blurt out, 'Don't worry dad, I will get you another grandson.'

At the time, I thought this was noble. Dad looked at me with surprise, but I'm not sure he was overly confident. In my nightly call with Ness after leaving his room I told her, 'By the way, we are having another child, it needs to be a boy.' This certainly took Ness by surprise. I had pretty much pulled up stumps on the thought of another child. Two seemed plenty for me. Ness was always keen on a third, so this news was not unwelcomed. The only problem being you cannot pre-order a son. I explained it had better be a boy, otherwise we needed to keep going until one arrived. This didn't go down too well, it must be said.

Although we were offered counselling over the few weeks we were in South Africa, I attended only two sessions. For me, whatever they were saying was going in one ear and out the other. I wanted Rob and the boys to be back and alive and talking about my feelings seemed pointless. Any mention of God, or that they were in heaven now, served only to irritate me. How would any God let this happen? This anger within kept bubbling away and it felt like I was going to burst. One of the counsellors asked what Rob meant to me. I still recall the look on her face after I blurted out various things while sobbing. She stared at me for a while and quietly said in her monotone South African accent, 'I see, he was nearly everything to you.'

This didn't help my state of mind, she wasn't helping as far as I was concerned. Looking back now I was being moronic. If I could go back in time, I would have continued counselling as much as I could. It would have made an enormous difference for the years to come. I know this now. But at the time I was plain stubborn, it seemed utterly useless for me.

The minister who conducted the funeral and his wife invited us over to his house the evening before we were due to fly out. Their property was surrounded by a huge fence and barbed wire. What a way to live, I thought as we drove in. They were such lovely people and very caring in how they treated us.

As we were leaving their house after dinner the minister's wife gave Don some pills. Not in a packet, just a couple of stand-alone pills. They knew we hadn't slept well for a few weeks and had the long flight home the next day. I remember being told, 'You guys should take one of these as the plane takes off, we guarantee it will put you into a deep sleep.'

Don accepted the pills and we thanked them for everything. Once in the car, I looked at the pills in his hand and said to Don, 'Surely they're dodgy.'

We didn't know what Dusty had planned in terms of a return to Australia. It would have been the last thing on her mind. We were comforted by the fact she was now in the hands of her own family. We would always be there for her, but she needed to be with her own family.

Dad, Don and I flew out of South Africa the next day. As we took off, I was thinking how glad I was to be going home to my own family and leaving this wretched land. Don asked if I was game enough to take one of the pills we had been given the night before. I would have taken anything to sleep so I was all for it. We had been served a couple of beers after take-off and he watched with a slight grin as I swigged down the pill. He clearly thought they might be dodgy, and appeared a little too keen to see what would happen. Dad sat across the aisle clutching three small boxes for the entire flight. The ashes of his son and grandsons.

CHAPTER 21

THE MEMORIAL

'Would you like some breakfast sir?' It was like a dream. Why was someone asking if I want breakfast in a dream? Then 'Whack,' I was hit with a solid punch to my arm that jolted me awake. I opened my eyes and found it was Don who had taken the swing... 'Wake up, dickhead,' he said with half a mouthful of toast. We were being served breakfast on the plane. I was stunned. That was quick. We were only an hour or so from landing. What the hell was going on? It took me a minute or two to get my bearings.

Don was laughing. 'You've been asleep since the moment you took that pill.'

'Really?' I couldn't believe it. Apparently not long after downing the pill I was fast asleep and remained that way for the whole trip. I've never slept on a plane as well I did this flight. 'Wow, I've no idea what it was but it worked,' I said groggily as the hostess set the breakfast tray down in front of me. I noticed the enquiring frown that crossed her face the mention of a pill. She must have thought we were on the gear, definitely.

It was the sleep I had desperately needed. For the first time in weeks. I felt I was half conscious. Soon we would be landing and have to face a press conference at the airport. I was far more ready to handle this now that I'd slept, so was feeling very grateful for whatever drug it was. We had heard bits and pieces while away about the impact of Rob and the boys' deaths back home in Melbourne, but I wasn't at all prepared for what we were about to face.

As soon as we arrived at Tullamarine airport, we were ushered into a conference room. Brian Walsh oversaw everything and led us through what was happening. Dad didn't want to have to front any cameras, so he quietly slid past and went home. Don and I answered questions as best as we could under the circumstances. We were then quickly ushered through Customs and baggage claim, again with the help and organisation from the AFL. Before we knew it, we were in our cars and driving home with our wives. It all happened so quickly and part of me felt like it was now all over.

Early that evening, Ness and I took Don and Di (Don's wife) to a local pizza place for dinner. For the briefest of moments, life felt very normal. Almost as if the last few weeks had never happened. It was pleasant. I started to feel a little relaxed for the first time in many days. It didn't last long. There was a television playing at the restaurant and the news came on. There were Don and I front and centre leading off the nightly news. Pictures of Rob and his boys were shown during the story and the brief moment of respite was gone. We couldn't hear the television, but the pictures said everything.

To see all the papers and news reports Ness had kept over the last few weeks came as a huge shock to me. I knew Rob was universally loved in the footy world, but he wasn't an A-grade player or huge name in the game by any means. But here he was, plastered all over the news media. I could only think he would have been thoroughly chuffed. He would have taken great delight in telling me he might have reached a solid B celebrity status.

The next few weeks were hectic. The AFL worked with me in planning a memorial service for Rob and the boys. It would be held at St Michael's Church in the city and the AFL would look after everything, including arranging a wake at the Melbourne Town Hall. It was incredible. Andrew Demetriou and his team were leaving no stone unturned. I wondered how many people would turn up for the memorial. It felt like all the planning was geared towards huge numbers. None of us knew how many would attend, so part of me was thinking this was all overkill.

Dusty's family had been in contact with dad from South Africa and let him know they would be travelling back to Australia in time for the memorial service. This was very welcome news. By now, I was running on adrenaline. I had promised dad I would take care of all the planning alongside the AFL for the service. He had done more than enough with his efforts for the funeral in South Africa. It became a huge distraction for me. I could escape the nightmare by keeping busy with the memorial and push everything else aside.

Part of my responsibility at the service would be to do the eulogy alongside Don. I was worried about this. How could I possibly talk about Rob in such a public setting? I could barely mention his name without breaking down. It was playing on my mind. The other task I had was to make a video tribute to be played at the close of the service. I delayed tackling it for as long as I could. The mere thought of looking at footage of Rob and the boys was too much to cope with. But time was fast approaching for the service and I had to get moving with it.

Most of Rob's footage of himself and the boys was spread over tapes and drives he kept in his office. The first time I walked back up those stairs again into his office was eerie to say the least. This was where I had said my last goodbyes to him only weeks earlier. I walked into his edit suite and sat at his desk, frozen. Rob was everywhere in here. The place was exactly as he had left it, typically a mess and unorganised. But it was calming in a way to sit there and feel his presence. I didn't know where to start. How could I do justice to them in a few days of editing? The adrenaline and tears were redlining for the next three days. I buried myself in all the footage and crafted a fifteen minute film. My whole focus was on what I thought Rob would like to watch. This is how I had always approached my work, and still do to this day.

Dusty and her family were back home a few days before the memorial. Our family all gathered with her on the morning of the service and were driven into the city and St Michael's Church. I was in the car with Dusty and as we neared the church we noticed the tide of people pouring up the steps to St

Michael's. The AFL was correct in its estimates. It was packed to the rafters and television cameras and photographers were spread all over the street outside. More than seven hundred people squeezed into the church. There was so much love for Rob and his boys.

My memories of the service are somewhat hazy. I was far too overcome with emotion to register much of what was happening. To be perfectly honest, I simply wanted it to be over. One of Rob's best friends from his primary school days, Colin Waddell, was the minister. He was perfect. The speakers, including some of Rob's mates and our family, all spoke beautifully. We had decided myself and Dusty would leave the church shortly before the end, avoiding the video tribute I had made. Dusty wasn't anywhere near ready to see the vision of her boys.

We left the church by the back door and went directly to the town hall. We sat quietly in a private room trying to regain some composure before everyone arrived for the wake. Dusty's strength was something to behold. If it had been me in her position, I wouldn't have been able to even get out of bed. She dragged herself up and made sure she was present for her three boys. Incredible strength. I was so proud of her.

Melbourne Town Hall was soon full of family and friends and people who knew Rob and the boys. There were so many who had only briefly met Rob through his films, such as *Essence of the Game* who turned up to pay their respects. This was the type of impact he had on people. On reflection, I think this is where I started to spiral downwards. It was so nice to see and hug family and friends and feel the love, no question.

But as the event went on, I started to mentally crumble. After such a draining day and trying to keep it all together I was becoming overwhelmed with sadness again. I just wanted to get the hell out of there and go home. This sounds ridiculous but to see people smiling and laughing was really annoying me. How could anyone be remotely happy? In hindsight this was so unfair and wrong of me to even think this way. People grieve and remember in their own way, which is as it should be. If this means laughing and smiling and recalling good memories, then so be it, more power to you. It's another safety mechanism in dealing with your own trauma. But for me, right at that moment, I was having none of it.

Someone organised an extended family photo of all our cousins. We hadn't been all together like this in many years, so it was a terrific opportunity for a photo. But to me, it just felt wrong. What are we doing here? Everyone smiling and happy posing for this picture. It really bothered me, but I stood there and took part. I have never seen the photo, but I assume I'm not exactly beaming.

I look back now and feel embarrassed about how I was feeling, especially when I think of the effort put in by so many to give Rob and the boys such a wonderful send-off. To everyone who attended and expressed their love and care for the family, how dare I feel this way. It's offensive. But it's how I felt, I couldn't escape it.

When the time came for us to leave the town hall and finally be done with the entire day, I couldn't depart fast enough. It was all over, and now I could go back to the coast and hide away from the world. The desire to be around people had gone, I was struggling to find the energy even to have conversations.

Once back in Point Lonsdale, I walked up to the back beach and sat in the dunes on what was a very windy day gazing out across the ocean. I started looking up at the clouds and kind of praying. Well, not praying as such, more like asking a few questions. If there was a God and Rob and the boys were up in heaven now, I wanted a sign. I wanted some proof. My brain was absorbed with questions like — where is heaven? Is it up in the sky? If so, then show me something in the clouds. It sounds like I was losing my mind, but all this was running through my head as I sat on the sand. I saw three clouds, oddly very close to each other, and tried to convince myself it was Rob, Gabriel and Byron giving me a sign. I desperately wanted to believe it was them, but it was ludicrous. I'd had enough of crying. I was teared out. My feeling now was one of pure anger more than anything else.

Like Rob, I was obviously raised in the same religious environment. Deep inside my soul I have always had a belief in God. No matter what I would get up to in life, in terms of non-Christian like activities, I never lost that internal belief there is something out there. I may not be living like mum would like me to be living, but it didn't mean I had totally forgotten all that I was taught as a child. She had instilled a morality in me which is permanent.

Walking back towards home across the top of the sand dunes, I was battling to believe in any of it. Rob and his two beautiful young boys were dead. Their whole lives were ahead, but had been stolen from them. It was too much for me to reconcile the fact that a god would let it happen. I began to understand why Rob might have been reading *The God Delusion* after all.

CHAPTER 22

AFL SEASON LAUNCH

For the next six months I became somewhat of a hermit. Other than concerns for Dusty, I didn't have too much contact with anyone other than family. I shut out a lot of people. I couldn't find the energy to engage. We were committed to do anything it took to help Dusty. Dad was enormous in getting all her affairs in order after Rob's passing, which was no easy feat with the mess he had left behind. Rob hadn't made a will, which was no real surprise. This kind of forward planning and administrative duty didn't interest him. He also had some significant taxation issues, so it was a huge task. Dad spent months working with a dear friend called Mike Williams, our accountant at the time, in trying to get everything in order.

Before the accident, I had been working on a small documentary for an AFL club. This was initially the only real work I managed to complete after returning from South Africa. Without realising it, I was starting to push all my grief to the side, or even into the background. It was too hard for the person I am to function. I'm not a morning person, and during this period I became fully aware I wasn't a mourning person either. Who is? But I'm far too emotional at the best of times. I was living in a constant state of unhappiness. What could I do to get out of this cycle, or even get five clear minutes a day when Rob didn't consume my thoughts?

Death is so final. You never get to see them again. It takes such a long time for it to really sink in, at times I feel it still hasn't sunk in all these years later. People move on with their lives and slowly but surely forget. It is the circle of life, but that it was all over for him and the boys was destroying me inside. He wouldn't be calling me anymore with his opening line mimicking the schoolteacher in his favourite movie, *Ferris Bueller's Day Off*. 'Anyone…Anyone…Anybody,' …it was ridiculous. It was his opening salvo in every single phone call to me for years. But it never got old, I loved it. Now I would look at my phone contacts list and stare at his name. I knew this number would never ring again. I still haven't deleted those digits from my phone. Just can't do it. For the first time in my life, I had a real affinity with those who had lost loved ones. I had lost grandparents and people who I was relatively close to, but this was different. I now understood what was going on behind the shattered faces of those who had lived this experience.

It was getting close to the 2009 AFL finals series, roughly four months since the accident. My mobile phone rang and I saw the caller was Danielle Bleazby from the AFL events team. I had come to know her through the memorial planning. Danielle went above and beyond to make it such a success, and I was so grateful to her. I still wasn't really answering the phone too much but this time I did. Dan wanted to know if I was interested in taking over the job of creating the season launch film, which Rob had so successfully produced over so many years.

Before he left for South Africa, he had told me in passing how he wanted me to do the next launch film. He thought he might have run his race with it and was suggesting maybe I have a crack. I'm not certain if he was deadly serious or would've changed his mind, but he was thinking about it. At the time, I was nonplussed. It was so far away I didn't give it another thought. But now, after everything that had happened, the AFL was asking if I wanted to take it on. It felt a bit ironic.

It was a request that scared the crap out of me. These Grand Final short films were in those days the centrepiece of the AFL season launch. It was a big deal. I remember Brendon Gale from the Richmond Football Club once telling me he only attended the event to watch the Grand Final films. My first thoughts were not exactly positive. If I took this on, would I destroy the whole night with a work of shit? Add in the fact that I might completely ruin Rob's legacy of brilliance with those films, meant I was not exactly thinking I was the right person for the job. It took some persuasion from Rob's team that worked with him filming the Grand Final each year, especially production manager Galia Hardy, to change my views. I realised they all wanted to continue what Rob had started as their own tribute to him.

After a few days deliberating I convinced myself Rob would

have wanted me to do it. I began to feel compelled to take it on. Even though I had been by Rob's side in and around the AFL scene since a teenager, part of me always felt like an outsider. Rob had played the game at the highest level. I hadn't. It wasn't that I was in awe of anyone or uncomfortable in their presence. I had grown up surrounded by AFL players and coaches through Rob, so they were always normal people to me. But when it came to the playing element I wasn't in the club. And it is a club, no doubt about that. If you've played senior AFL footy, you're in it, if you haven't, you're not. I wasn't sure how I would be received in the inner sanctum of clubs now that Rob was not here. This made me more nervous than the idea of creating the short films for the launch.

As part of what I was making for the event, I proposed an idea to make a second lighter type piece involving the coaches. It would be seen only by those in the room and not for public consumption. It was a piss-take where all the coaches would mimic along to a Black-Eyed Peas track, showing another side of them. The Premiership Cup was the centrepiece, and the idea was they were all chasing to get their hands on it. It was slightly left field, and I didn't hold much hope the coaches would be interested in taking part.

I proceeded to contact all the coaches with the concept. This is when it really hit home the impact Rob had on a lot of these men. Without hesitation, when they knew it was Rob's brother calling, they agreed to do whatever I wanted. It was amazing. I knew probably half a dozen of them personally already, so they were always going to help. And I've no doubt receiving such a positive response from those I didn't know was purely because of Rob. They trusted Rob and therefore believed they should be able to trust me. Each one of them was welcoming, warm, and embraced me. They would never have known how important their attitude towards me helped ease some of my insecurities. Some offered helpful insights and advice about losing a family member. Mark 'Chocko' Williams grabbed me as soon as I got to the Port Adelaide oval and wanted to know how I was, his whole focus was on me. He talked to me about losing his younger brother years earlier, and said he knew how I was feeling. He was just so caring. I still remember him saying, 'It never leaves you Pete, I still think of him and miss him daily.' Ross Lyon was another who gave me so much support. I have similar stories for all the coaches. It was overwhelming.

The start of the 2010 AFL season was now only a week away. The AFL invited me and the family, including Dusty, to attend the season launch evening. I was petrified. It was so emotional to be there. Fortunately, everything went as well as I could have ever wished. The films were a hit, and I sank into my seat in pure relief. Being told by those who attended that it had Rob written all over it gave me some joy. I hadn't felt joy in many months. There was a real connection to Rob for people through what I had made. In my mind it was nowhere near his level of quality, but it had least opened a new way of thinking for me. It gave me a purpose. I was going to go as hard as I possibly could in making films which would keep Rob's legacy alive. If people continued to see work similar to what he had produced, it might remind them of Rob, and in a way keep him present.

This is what I began to convince myself of anyway. I cringe now for ever thinking in such a way, but I wasn't processing things rationally. I realise all I was doing was trying to find a way out of the constant pain. This was my escape, keeping a crazed legacy as my focus. I created this in my own mind. It would become a manic quest.

CHAPTER 23

AFL HOUSE

'I've just had the scan,' she said. I was on the other end of the phone barely able to speak. I was incredibly nervous waiting on what she would say next. Ness had taken a trip into Melbourne for a scan to determine the sex of our soon to be third child. 'It's a boy.' I could hear the emotion in her voice. We had wanted a healthy newborn, regardless of the sex. But after my slightly unstable promise to dad, there was no doubt we had more than a modest leaning towards having a boy this time. It was magical. On 29 May 2010, our son Luke Robert Kingsley Dickson was born. Luke was a very welcome addition to the Dickson clan. Dad was especially joyous. Ness was full of relief, probably more because I wouldn't be pushing for a fourth child.

Following the build-up and response to the season launch film, I slowly started to get myself back into working on various projects. Things were ticking along slowly workwise, without anything major being offered. My ideal plan was to create longer form documentaries, as I had experienced with Rob. So, when Sam Walch, head of AFL Media, gave me a call for a chat, I was intrigued. We met for a coffee and I instantly liked him, we had a great rapport. At the time he was working directly under Gillon McLachlan. His focus was to build AFL Media from the ground up. Sam was very keen to get me on board as an employee to create content for the new entity. It was the first time since I had started working with Rob that an opportunity had arisen to work for someone else. By now I was firmly entrenched in the mindset of being an independent, work for myself type of operator. This contributed to my reluctance to accept Sam's offer. I drove him mad. But eventually the lure of steady, regular income became too hard to decline. More importantly, the opportunities of working within the AFL system itself were infinitely more abundant than battling for funding out on my own.

It was a hot and steamy Sunday afternoon in January 2011. I was due to start my new role at AFL House the very next day. I was apprehensive about starting a real job again. The idea of being an employee with a boss wasn't exactly thrilling me. But I had to grab the opportunity and viewed it as a chance to develop my storytelling skills further. The Dickson kids had always worked for themselves. All of us. Makes you think we might possibly have some issues with authoritarian type figures. I've no idea why. I think it must have had something to do with our childhood experiences, but we've all much preferred working independently. With this edginess about starting with the AFL the next day, it was a pleasant distraction to play some cricket on this balmy Sunday afternoon.

Asked to fill in alongside some old cricket buddies for the fourth eleven at my old club, Malvern, I was excited about having a hit and spanking some twelve-year-olds around the park. We fielded first. Having not played for six years, I was fully aware my hamstrings could ping at any stage and was reluctant to put too much effort into fielding. Instead, I was casually using my feet to stop any balls heading my way. I did this once too often and plonked my right foot directly on top of one, causing my ankle to give way. I hit the deck hard. Fellow teammates were rolling around the turf in fits of laughter.

I soon had to do the walk of shame off the field to put some ice on the now inflamed ankle. I received stinging sledges from past players watching, 'Toughen up nancy boy' was still ringing in my ears two hours later as I entered Cabrini Hospital with a fractured ankle. I was immediately booked in for an operation to insert a pin into the bones. Perfect. Full of embarrassment I made a phone call to my new boss Sam Walch requesting a delayed beginning to my new gig. Off to a cracking start. I'm sure he thought what the hell have we done hiring this nancy boy.

My first day working at the AFL finally arrived a month after my operation. Because I was a sole operator, I had taken all my own gear with me. The AFL Media area was still being formed and it felt easier for me to bring all my own computers and monitors and be set up immediately. It also gave me the feeling I was still doing my own thing, not relying on AFL equipment to operate. I felt totally out of place at AFL House the moment I walked in. For some reason I can't explain it felt wrong. I was on crutches and in a moon boot, battling to even get around. For the first few weeks I felt like I was back in my youth, going to a new school. You think everyone is staring at you and whispering behind your back. This was how it felt, even though I'm pretty sure no one gave me a second glance. I knew several staff quite well already through work over the years so that helped immensely.

They put me in a little area which I referred to as 'the cave.' It was in a corner on the second floor of AFL House and was just for me. I liked that. Sitting in an open office situation with desks and people in close proximity was not something on which I was all that keen. When you're editing it doesn't work, you need your own space.

One of my first projects was to be a thirty-minute documentary on the St Kilda Football Club. Two of the senior people in AFL Media at the time, Greg Miles and Ian Weeding, had been in discussions with the club about the prospect of a documentary. I attended a meeting with them and the St Kilda hierarchy during my first week. Ross Lyon was the coach. The club had suffered a drawn Grand Final draw against Collingwood, followed by a replay, which they lost. It was now pre-season, and the documentary would be called *The Challenge*. It would take a deep look within the inner sanctum of the club, and how it was preparing for season 2011. It would examine and flesh out the challenge of rebounding from the heartbreak of the season before.

Michael Nettlefold, the CEO, and Ross Lyon were magnificent in opening the club to me and a couple of my freelancers, Lincoln Cleak and Justin Powell. I had full access and, still hobbling around on crutches, would spend nearly two weeks embedded with the players and coaches at their Seaford base. Players and coaches were still hurting. Two close Grand Final defeats in two years were gut wrenching to deal with. To gain this access at such a brutal time as they tried to get themselves up for another season was unique. Ross told me we could attend all the meetings, take as much footage as we needed, speak to anyone including himself for interview content, and basically do as much as we pleased. He said he trusted me with all that content. I promised him that anything not used for the film would be returned to him alone. He was happy with that. For my part, I felt deeply duty bound to do the right thing by him and the club. I was in the initial stages of this manic mode of ensuring that the trust Rob had built over so many years within clubland stayed alive. I was working for Ross and the players, not the AFL. This was my mindset.

After a whirlwind month or two, I finished cutting a draft of *The Challenge*, which was when things got a little messy within the walls of AFL House. I had given Ross and the leadership group a couple of viewings of the film to establish what they were comfortable with staying in or taking out. My whole focus was on ensuring I didn't release anything against their wishes. By the time I got around to showing the AFL a draft, it was already signed off by Ross Lyon and the club.

My style of storytelling was (and still is) very much in the mould of non-voiceover. Rob and I always thought it was cheating. Of course, it's not, many documentaries simply demand having a narrator. But for this film I was adamant the craft of the storytelling was strong enough to carry without need for a voiceover. It presents a real challenge (pardon the pun) to make a film flow and tell a compelling story without needing a scripted voice over the top. It means you have done the work. I'm not saying it's the right way or the wrong way, but for me, it's the way I prefer to craft a narrative. Ross and the leadership of the club agreed entirely, they didn't want it voiced either. But there were others who had a different view.

'We are having a screening of your draft in room such and such at 2 pm' I was told by one of the AFL executives of the time. No worries, I thought, they will love it. The content within the film for that era was rarely if ever seen in public, so I was certain they would be delighted with the result. As I entered the meeting room for the screening, I was stunned to see at least twelve people sitting around a huge table. For a moment I thought I was in the wrong place. But no, they were all there for a viewing. I'm thinking, 'Okay, so this is interesting. Why so many people?'

They were all from different departments and areas of expertise, but only one or two in the room would vaguely know anything about making a documentary. It immediately felt like a firing squad. The niceties at the start were soon over and they played the film. I was taking the odd look around the table as the film played and was noticing furious note taking by many in the room. I'm thinking wow, what's all this? The doco ended and there was an awkward silence, no one really knew who would begin speaking. One of the more senior people in the room suggested we go around the table and listen to the views and changes required by each person.

I was simply stunned. Why would I listen to the views of someone who might be from accounts and make the changes they demanded? No disrespect to accounts, it could just as well be any other department, but unless they had made some documentaries before then I was not really interested in their opinion. I might as well go outside and ask Joe Blogs off the street to view it and tell me what needed changing.

For the next fifteen minutes I sat quietly fuming listening to person after person give their opinions. I've been told numerous times my face doesn't have the ability to hide what I'm thinking. I can only assume everyone was fully aware of what I was thinking. I was deciding this was not for me. You cannot make this type of film by committee. Especially a committee without any experience or understanding of crafting a film together. What am I doing here if they don't trust me as a filmmaker? This is my job. I wasn't sitting around a table reviewing their own work in their departments, that's not my area. To me, this was all bullshit. Some of the older school types in the room thought it needed a scripted voiceover. Of course, I thought to myself, I knew that was coming. Not long after the last member of the group scrutinised the film, the meeting was finally wrapped up. I left the room and departed AFL House. I decided to get the hell out of there, this wasn't going to work for me.

This role I was undertaking and subsequent style of documentary making was new to the AFL. It was fresh, and for other employees it was intoxicating to see it happening. I was told this numerous times by many within the AFL. Part of me felt it was something everyone wanted to somehow be involved with if they could. Fair enough.

Most people working for the AFL passionately love the game. They were seeing things such as the inside workings of a club at firsthand, all fans of the game want to see this kind of content. Most of those in the meeting were all great people keen to somehow be involved, and this was a way of doing so. I had no animosity towards any of them whatsoever. I understood it.

I had a chat about what had just taken place with Galia Hardy, one of Rob and my mentors. I trusted her advice. She, too, thought it was utterly ridiculous. 'Respect and listen to a couple of voices you trust and who know what they're talking about. Anything outside of this is just noise.'

It was the message I needed to hear, it made me think I wasn't being a stubborn, moody, dickhead. Although there was certainly an element of dickhead going on. Unbeknown to me, Galia called her great friend Ross Lyon a few hours later to discuss what we had spoken about.

'Are you a little grumpy mate?'

It was Ross Lyon on his car phone en-route to Seaford the next day.

'Let me guess, Gags has spoken with you hasn't she,' I responded. He laughed and said, 'Maybe.' The subsequent chat with Ross really helped my state of mind. I think of it now and believe it was exactly what I needed. He reiterated the advice to trust my instincts. He thought the film captured the mood and current reality of the club perfectly. He was really proud of it.

Ross was fully aware I had severe doubts about my ability as a filmmaker. He knew full well how I kept comparing myself to Rob and he would tell me often to let that go. He knew what a meeting of that nature would be doing to my confidence. There were still a few subtle changes I had to make which the club were keen on, but otherwise his view was that it was finished. They didn't want to hear any wanky voiceover, they didn't want anything else to be added or taken out, as far as they were concerned it was done. I found myself in a little bit of a bind, caught serving two masters.

I then had a chat with Sam Walch and Gillon McLachlan who were both somewhat surprised at hearing of the viewing. Neither had been present. I suggested it would be best if I finished up after finalising the film. I let them know I wasn't changing the film other than doing what St Kilda had requested. If the AFL wanted to change it, let someone else do it, but I wouldn't be doing it myself.

I've no doubt they both thought I was being petulant, and I probably was. Gill in his laid-back manner was laughing and bagging me as he does for being too precious. Probably telling me this for at least the hundredth time over the years, 'You Dicksons are hard work aren't you?'

Maybe I was, but for me this process was not something I was keen on going through for every film made. If this was the way things operated in the AFL, it wasn't for me. When you work for yourself, it's all down to you. I'm happy to accept the good and the bad with this responsibility. I'd rather live and die by my own decisions. I was and still am a firm believer that you can't do this by committee. I'm happy to take the views from a close few who I have absolute faith in for their ability and experience. But outside of this, no. I get so emotionally invested in the storytelling and often feel like it's my baby.

I was more than happy to go back out on my own. The reality was that I was probably trying to escape again. Escape criticism or doubts over my ability. This was an easy reason for convincing myself why I should leave. I kept thinking back to Rob and his reactions when Channel Seven critiqued *The Essence of the Game* and wanted to change it. Now here was me now reacting in the same way. Birds of a feather.

'Nope.' Gill was wrapping up our conversation. 'No way, stick at it, we'll work it all out.'

He was adamant this was all a storm in a teacup and the natural order of things would slowly evolve with the role I was doing. He was correct. Annoyingly. Gill had so much faith and support for me. One of the main reasons I stayed on was because of him. He knew what buttons to press with me, that's for certain. He still does.

As the months progressed, I was given more freedom, or as much as was possible within the AFL system, to create documentaries. I never had to undergo a panel of twelve critics again. Mostly I had a couple of senior people in AFL Media, or broadcast network people, as the people I would trust to view and help sign off work going forward. This worked for me, and it worked for them.

The Challenge was released on Channel Nine, my first feature documentary to get a broadcast release without Rob. I had compromised a tiny bit by allowing a voiceover at the very beginning. I didn't think it added anything but pick your battles, I thought. St Kilda and their fans loved it, and Ross got all the excess inner sanctum footage back.

CHAPTER 24

FIFTY OF YOU

For the next eighteen months, I threw myself completely into making football documentaries for the AFL. First there was *2 Hours*, the story of the 2011 Grand Final, which aired on Channel Seven. We then embarked on a TV series called *The Final Story*. We would go back in time and document epic Grand Finals and those who played and coached in each game. The AFL had brought in a freelance documentary maker, Wayne Dyer, to help me with the workload. He was the first person I had really worked closely with on documentary films since Rob died. Wayne was terrific for me. He was an old school structured documentary maker. His methods were very unlike mine. But I learnt so much from him. It allowed me to take a critical look at how I was crafting and going through the process. Some things I took on board, others didn't suit me, but it was enlightening.

As a family, we had moved back to live in Melbourne permanently. Juggling this new position where I would be away from home a lot, with a baby and two young children, and a wife working on-call full time was challenging to say the least. It meant I was spending very little time reflecting on Rob or dealing with the grief lurking below the surface. You don't think like this at the time and I thought I was doing okay in that department. But I wasn't.

Unashamedly my favourite *Final Story* was the 1989 Grand Final. It meant digging into the game for which Rob missed selection and had such a profound effect on his life. Spending time with his old teammates again was both fun and difficult. Their love for Rob and their own stories of missing him were profound. Being the director gave me some freedom to weave Rob into the narrative. If I look at it pragmatically, I probably spent a little too long on his story within the story. But what the hell, I thought, I'm making the film so bugger it.

This production was a strange experience. On reflection, I realise I went into another zone, removing my own emotions completely and treating Rob like he was just another element and character within the story. If I focussed even a little too much on him from a brother's viewpoint, I would not have been able to do what was needed. Being well versed in pushing my feelings of grief into the background, this was another example of keeping this stuff well buried.

Once I completed the doco the AFL launched the film at Crown Casino's cinema. Most of the players from both teams were in attendance and the cinema was full. Sitting in such environments watching my own work among an audience viewing it for the first time is gut-wrenching. I hate it. If people don't react the way I would hope during the screening it bites at me. It sounds like a wonderful thing to be part of, and it really is, and I've been extremely lucky to have had these screenings and launches for many of my productions. But as the director your efforts are now there for all to see, and you're sitting right there in amongst them. If it bombs, there is nowhere to hide. Stress levels are high. It irks me that I feel that way. I would love to soak these moments in and simply enjoy the experience, but it's impossible for me to do that.

Thankfully, this one was well received. The relief I felt hearing the audience burst into clapping and cheers at the final credits was something I will never forget. His old teammates and opponents loved it, which was all that mattered to me. All you want is for them to feel it was an accurate portrayal of their story. I remember leaving the cinema and Gill bailing me up to say, 'Well done.' As he departed, he laughed and said, 'I can't believe you pulled it off … a film on the best Grand Final ever, which was basically a tribute to Rob.' I couldn't really argue with him.

'You know I have about fifty of you.' It was some months later and I was sitting in the Channel Seven boardroom on a couch alongside Peter Campbell, the new head of AFL Media, and Simon Lethlean, the AFL's head of broadcasting. Opposite us was a Seven Network executive who had just said something that triggered me no end.

'Sorry, what was that'? I said to him. He repeated it, 'Mate, you know I have fifty of you don't you'?

I couldn't believe it. It was so confronting. We were in the boardroom discussing my new documentary, *The Chosen Few*. This was a concept which would have me spend twelve months with all the AFL coaches and produce a behind the scenes film of what life as an AFL coach was really like. We were talking with the network to see if it might be interested in taking the film for broadcast once finished.

I had spent the preceding few months with great friend Danny 'Spud' Frawley discussing this concept. Spud was the head of the AFL Coaches Association and instrumental in getting this project off the ground. He had invited me to an AFL coaches' dinner a few months earlier to pitch the idea to all the coaches. We were in a Sydney restaurant and I was absolutely shitting myself. It was one tough room. But with the support from Danny and the AFL, all the coaches agreed to take part. It would be my biggest undertaking yet as a solo filmmaker. Ninety minutes of prime-time TV.

'Really?' I said to the Channel Seven executive. 'Not sure about that,' said Peter Campbell, trying his best to support me.

This was my first real heavyweight meeting with a network. Up until now the AFL had managed to strike deals themselves without much pitching from me. This was different. It was a huge undertaking and would cost plenty to make. The AFL was looking for a financial partner in the production, which explains why we were sitting in the network's boardroom.

The executive's comment floored me. I honestly cannot remember much more of the meeting afterwards. For the first time in a long time, the doubts of whether I was any good at this caper had resurfaced. Every time I had released a documentary since Rob's passing, I would think how I might be edging a little closer to his standard. The fact I considered him the best in the business, meant I thought I might be up around that mark. But not according to this guy. If this network believed they had fifty of me what the hell was I doing in this meeting? I kept thinking if it was Rob sitting here, there was no way they would say that. The insecurities I had tried to suppress over the last eighteen months or so were bubbling up.

As we walked back to AFL House, it's fair to say I was all over the shop. 'Fuck him, let them do it themselves if there are fifty of them who can.'

I was steaming. Simon was doing his best to calm me down. 'Chill mate — it's all part of the game.' He explained how they were trying to downplay how much they would have to contribute financially. To him, it was familiar tactic. From my viewpoint, I was always under the impression that Channel Seven detested AFL Media. It believed AFL Media was trampling on its territory, and I always felt it gave scant respect to anything coming out of there. Hearing it say it had fifty of me in there was not totally unexpected.

No offence to the people in the network at the time, but I didn't know of anyone producing and directing documentaries at the level we were achieving. Maybe they were, but I had never seen one. As we entered AFL House, Peter Campbell said, 'Even if they had fifty of you Pete, which they don't, the coaches would still want you to do it, not them.'

I went back to my edit suite and reflected on this comment for a long while, it was true. But was it because I was any good at making films, or was I simply being handed the mantle after Rob died because I was his brother? That sledge received an hour earlier had cemented in my heart that it was purely because I was Rob's brother. I was already treading a rocky path in trying to be his equal, accepted and known as a decent storyteller, like he was. It's pretty hard to keep walking the path with any confidence when you hear there are fifty more of you just metres up the road.

Why could I not do my best and accept it would be good enough? Why did I get so worked up about all this? It was eating away at me as well as pushing me to do more. Not a very healthy mix. I knew no one cared about any of this, wouldn't have even given it a second thought. It was all in my own mind. But I couldn't let it go. This is when I first started to feel like something was seriously amiss with me.

CHAPTER 25

WHAT NOW?

'I think I'm done mate.' I was sitting in the office of Gillon McLachlan, now the AFL CEO. This was a discussion with Gill I had put off for far too long because I didn't want him to be disappointed in me. Having completed what would be my last feature documentary for the AFL *The Final Draw*, based on the 2010 Grand Final between St Kilda and Collingwood, I was well and truly cooked. In the two years before this release I had made *The Chosen Few*, Life *of an AFL Coach*, as well as *The Chosen Few 2, Life of an AFL Captain*. Both were ninety-minute feature broadcast documentaries that eventually ended up on Channel Seven, even though they apparently had fifty of me in there who could have made the films. I had lived the process 24/7 and thrown everything I had into making those documentaries. There was nothing left in the tank.

'What's going on big guy?' Gill asked with a slightly concerned expression.

He had definitely picked up on me sliding backwards over the last year or so. One thing I know about Gill is that he cares about people. Since I'd first met him all those years ago it was a trait clearly evident within him.

Since Rob had died, he was always checking in on me, always ensuring I was going okay.

'It's time for me to leave the AFL,' I answered.

'Now why would you do that? Do you have another job or project in the works out there?'

'Ummm no....'

'Then why leave?'

He was a somewhat annoyed. There were so many reasons I needed a change it was hard to give him a direct answer. The fact that for months I had been waking up with the shakes was playing on my mind, something had to change in my life. I knew he didn't care that I wouldn't be working at AFL House anymore, he merely wanted to ensure I would be okay.

After a long and emotional chat, we agreed it was best to part ways. He understood and was typically supportive of whatever I felt was best for me. There would be some ongoing small projects here and there I would continue to do for a while externally, but not full-time employment. Within a few weeks I had quietly departed the offices of AFL House. I doubt anyone even noticed I wasn't around anymore.

When I think about my years within the AFL, I think of the relationships and opportunities I was given to be front and centre at the heart of the game. It was almost as if this was compensation for not being able to play because of my kidneys.

I was blessed to be present in the inner sanctum of every club at some point. The access I was granted was as close as you could possibly get to being a player without being a player. You become so immersed in the system you feel part of it. Even though you are clearly not, there is definitely a sense of belonging to the footy family. That is what I reflect on as the best part of those years. My initial fears about being accepted, not being Rob Dickson, not being anywhere nearly as talented as him, would slowly subside, but not disappear completely. I couldn't have been welcomed and trusted any more than I was. It was incredible and I'm forever grateful to everyone who backed me following Rob's death.

One thing which had changed within was my tolerance for football content. By the time I left, there was saturation coverage of the game and stories surrounding the game. Fox Footy, Channel Seven, AFL Media, radio and many other platforms all seemingly doing the same thing.

Each year would roll around and it would all be the same, maybe different faces and voices but essentially the same. New voice-overed packages of hype which in essence are mirror images of what was produced the year before. Interviews from clubs 'we will be pushing hard for finals this year...we think we're good enough...and 'I'm backing our skipper in for a bumper year this year, his pre-season has been unbelievable' ...okay, might have heard this last year, and the year before.

I know they have to say something, but I couldn't listen to any more of it. It's a very rare occasion for a club or player to say something that doesn't sound scripted by their own media department. I know the game needs the media to survive so I understand it's necessary, and most fans crave it. But having been immersed in it for so long I became jaded by the whole circus and it was clearly time for me to do something else. I needed to venture into other sports, create content for anything but the AFL. I still loved the game, but storytelling wise I had exhausted what I wanted to do in this space.

The mystique and mystery of sport and talent is what excites me. I enjoy making films featuring people you've rarely if ever heard speak before. The enigma. Unfiltered. These days we know everything instantly, it is all there daily, hourly, relentless coverage feeding the beast.

A few weeks later, I was sitting alone on my back deck with Ness at work and the kids at school. I had anticipated after leaving I would start to relax, maybe begin to wind down a little.

Unfortunately, the opposite happened. My brain was still working in overdrive. I wasn't sleeping. Before starting at the AFL, I only really knew one method of working. You pick up a project, be paid for the project and hope for another one soon. You are fully aware it may take some time to pick up another one. It's a never-ending cycle. But having experienced the stability of a constant wage and the level of security the AFL offered, I had kind of forgotten what working for oneself was like. This was scary. Would anyone ever again ask me to make a film? What the hell was I going to do now? The reality of the decision I had made to leave, felt like it had smacked me in the face. The other problem was that I was again spending a great deal of time thinking about Rob. Now that I wasn't in a work frenzy like I had been over recent years, he was starting to be on my mind, more and more.

CHAPTER 26

FORGED IN FIRE

It was now 2016, my daughter Abby was in Grade Six, and one day in class she wrote a poem to me. This poem was profound in so many ways for a girl of her age to write. It drove home to me how my grief had spilled over into those around me, especially my own kids. This was what she wrote...

I was only very small and young,
when the sad news bounced off my tongue.
The news that left my dad in pain,
the special people that do not remain.
I was too young to understand,
I wish they were still standing on this land.
The people who said they would have been fun,
to the sad thought of saying goodbye.
Not knowing about them at all,
I'm not running off to have a ball.

The news that breaks anyone's heart,
Them and I are now apart.
The pain of seeing his pale face,
is harder than running a race.
I don't remember anything,
The photos tell me everything.
The vehicle that you drive around,
That has a quiet engine sound,
Is the reason for this tragedy,
No one will get through it casually.
A tragedy that no man can save,
but you still have to stay brave,
he's famous till today,
you'll see him in a photo one day.
The end has to come with everyone,
some grandparents have said goodbye to their grandson.
He could be young or old,
but it leaves a spot in your heart that's cold.
Everyone faces a sad goodbye,
the same as I.

It stunned me to read it. Even at such a young age, she was being deeply affected, something that concerned me immensely. The last thing I wanted was my children to carry scars from my own behaviour. It was an extreme reality check for me to try to be more present and upbeat around them. I'm not sure I succeeded to any great heights, but this poem at least opened my eyes to what was being witnessed by those closest to me.

While trying to re-establish my own business away from AFL headquarters, I had decided to rename my production company as Dickson Films. This was because I wanted to incorporate Rob into the mix. I wanted a place where I could showcase all his works as well as mine.

Dickson Films was an obvious name choice. At the time, an article appeared in one of the Melbourne papers about this, and how Rob's films would be available via my new website. It didn't take long for me to start getting messages saying it sounded like a porn site. Dicks…on…Films. Totally juvenile, but I had never even considered this was how it read. Geeshh, so it does too, I thought. Oh well, bad luck, I was keeping the name. Those who see something else in the name must have dirty minds.

'Hi, is this Peter Dickson?' a voice on the other end of the phone asked. It was late in 2016 and any call I received was potentially some project work, so I was unusually keen on taking any calls at the time.

'Yes, it is,' I responded. I hadn't heard this voice before.

'Hi, my name is Richard Ostroff and I work with Cricket Australia.'

When I heard the words Cricket Australia, it was like I had time travelled back into their Jolimont offices in the early 2000s.

Not long after we had finished our first documentary, *The Passion to Play* back in 2002, Rob, Hamish McLachlan, and I found ourselves presenting a proposal to the heads of Cricket Australia in a very small meeting room in their Jolimont building. We had gotten to know Hamish very well through Gill, and by working on the Hall of Fame project. He was a slick and polished presenter. We needed a bit of shine in the presentation stakes so asked if he wouldn't mind coming along with us. He was more than happy to help us out. We were a little intimidated by Cricket Australia back then, I'm not sure why, but I know for Rob it was out of his comfort zone. With the success of *The Passion to Play* I had suggested to him that we should do something similar for cricket. Rob wasn't a huge fan of cricket, but he knew it was a sport I loved and said, 'Sure why not, you put together a proposal and outline and we should set up a meeting.' So here we were a month or so later, listening to Hamish try to sell our idea to three suited up, very serious looking gentlemen.

'Thank you for your time guys, fantastic concept and presentation, leave it with us and we will get back to you over the next few weeks,' said one of the CA suits.

As we were leaving and walking down the stairs outside, I said, 'Maybe we should have worn suits.' Rob scoffed, 'Pfftt, I don't even have one.' Of course, I thought, what a stupid statement. A few weeks later a letter arrived from Cricket Australia. It was not keen but thanked us again for making an effort with the proposal. I was very disappointed. Cricket was my game and to have an opportunity to be involved in telling its history and that of the players who have graced its fields was beyond exciting for me back then. But it fell flat. I'm certain Rob wasn't too fussed as he had a lot more left to do in the AFL world.

So when I received this call from Cricket Australia in 2016 I was very surprised. Richard was ringing to see if I was interested in meeting him for a coffee and a chat. He was the commercial manager, media rights and broadcast for CA.

'Love to,' I said.

Richard was very personable, and I enjoyed his company. He wanted to see if I was interested in doing some documentary storytelling for Cricket Australia. He, along with Ben Amarfio, who was the executive general manager of broadcasting and commercial, were in the very early stages of establishing their own media arm within Cricket Australia. It was not dissimilar to what the AFL had set up with AFL Media.

I had known Ben for a long time through the AFL network, so I was extremely keen to get involved with what they were doing. After a few months of back and forth and discussions on what they were looking for in a feature documentary, we signed an agreement for me to make *Forged in Fire, Cricket's Greatest Rivalry*. This would be a three-part TV series for the Channel Nine network, telling the story of Ashes cricket.

Richard was instrumental in getting this off the ground. He had approached me only a few months earlier and here we were already in partnership making a feature documentary. He and Ben deserve much credit for making it happen. When I signed the contract, I kept thinking of Rob and how pleased he would be I finally had a chance to make a film on cricket.

It was exciting but also daunting. This was three hours of national TV. It was an enormous undertaking to be completed in not the longest of timeframes. I had my usual freelance team all set and ready to go, as well as a new addition in production manager Mel Mullen. We would attempt to interview most of the current and past Australian cricketers we had selected first, before flying off to England to interview their Ashes counterparts.

I felt re-energised and excited about venturing into this fresh territory of storytelling, and an altogether different code. It again allowed me to temporarily remove myself from the whole Rob situation, which was still lying in wait.

For someone who grew up idolising cricketers this was something new for me. The difference I immediately found when interviews started was that I was somewhat star struck. In football, I didn't have this feeling at all, with anyone. I put it down to being surrounded by AFL players from an early age when Rob started playing with Hawthorn. But this was different, these were people who I'd never had contact with and, in a way, were almost mythical. I quickly realised I had to park that straight away. Be professional, don't be a fanboy, do your job.

Ben and Richard were highly involved in most decisions pertaining to the film from the get-go. This was also something very different for me. For the last few years, I had total autonomy in all my documentaries, but they were all over this one. Me being me I pushed back on this as much as I could. 'Just leave me to it,' was my overriding attitude at the time, but with this being a fresh environment for me, a fresh organisation, I had to try to do my best to accommodate them being involved as much as they could. I sensed early on they were a little annoyed at my arm's length style of operating. There was so much to do and it was very much a case of where do I start? To get myself into the swing of interviewing cricketers and gain some handy insights from someone I already knew, I called Damien Fleming.

I first met 'Flem' back in 2005. It was my last season of playing sub-district cricket with Malvern. I was captain of the first eleven and my team had pretty much sauntered through the whole year undefeated. Flem was playing for Noble Park that season for what must have been plenty of the 'folding stuff'. He wasn't far removed from playing for Victoria and Australia and this level of cricket was a nice step down for him. He was a big fish in a little pond.

We finished the season on top, Noble Park barely snuck into sixth place and scraped into the finals. We breezed through the finals and so did Noble Park. As it turned out, we both made the Grand Final which was played at our home ground in Malvern. We bowled first and managed to dismiss them for around 145. We had one hand on the trophy, was what we were thinking. We were absolutely bursting with confidence as a team following the season we had had.

There were still seventeen overs of play left in the day, which bothered me a tad as captain. I wanted us to get through to stumps without many wickets lost so we could wrap it up the next day. Well, you could say things took a turn.

Flem was going to give his bowling career one final serious crack. He steamed in and the ball was hooping all over the place, the bowler at the other end was also doing the same. Seeing my guys' faces who were waiting to bat as Flem was going about his business, wasn't instilling me with great hope. They were clearly thinking of the Australian bowler Damien Fleming, not Flem from Noble Park.

When it was my turn at the crease, I think I had nearly top scored with three runs when Flem bowled me a quick bouncer directly at the badge of my helmet. I swayed out of the way thinking all was well; I had him covered. No drama here. The very next ball he bowled the same delivery...but at least 20 km/h faster, or that's what it felt like. I barely got a glove on it to protect myself and it slowly popped up to first slip. Out. The last ball I would ever face in anger, in half serious cricket. At stumps we were something like nine for sixteen. Yes, nine wickets down. Game over. Humiliation. The next day we scraped some more runs, but it was fruitless. Flem was supreme and showed everyone watching why he had the career he did. He could hardly walk the next morning, he looked like he had torn both hamstrings by the way he was moving from his all his efforts, which only made me think if we still had wickets in the shed how different the result might have been. But money well spent, Noble Park, and well played.

Rob was filming some of the action and he already knew Flem well. I talked with them both post game and told Rob the footage would never see the light of day. Flem was desperate to get hold of it, but I never allowed it to happen. Might have been still a little salty at this stage.

So, my first *Forged in Fire* interview was conducted with Damien Fleming at my house. He was superb and it really set the tone for what was to come. He wanted me to somehow weave the nine for sixteen story into the film. I respectfully declined.

What I soon found out when the interviewing process began, was that most of the past Australian cricketers had no time for Cricket Australia. This was different from past AFL players and their views on the AFL. In my experience if a past AFL player had an opinion at all, it wasn't necessarily scathing. But cricket was a different beast. So many of the players I contacted had no interest in doing anything for Cricket Australia, I don't think there was anything specific, they all seemed to have their personal reasons, but it was a hard grind to entice them to take part. The fact I didn't work for Cricket Australia and was an independent filmmaker certainly helped sway those who did take part. But it was a huge shock encountering these attitudes at the time.

The main anti-Cricket Australia types were the older generation of players. My good friend Bruce Eva, a prominent cricket commentator and journalist, was assisting me in trying to line up some of the past players he knew personally. One of those was Ian Chappell. It's fair to say in his interview he didn't hold back in his views on any topic. It ran for nearly three hours. He then demanded Bruce and I and the team have dinner and drinks with him. I think I'm still hungover today, he drank me under the table that's for sure.

It was such a rollicking experience for a cricket lover to spend time with all these legends. I remember walking around the back of Doug Walters' house to find him lounging in what looked like a home-made TAB. He had television screens everywhere with different horse races on each. An amazing set-up. Such a gentleman who absolutely lived up to the myth I had of him in my head.

The late Shane Warne also delivered in spades. He already had a contract with Channel Nine so even though he detested Cricket Australia, he felt obliged to take part due to it being aired on his channel. When I arrived at his Brighton mansion, he opened the front gate with a cigarette firmly nestled behind each ear. Brilliant. It was mesmerising to see him take regular breaks during our interview to suck down a durry. I had never seen someone smoke so many cigarettes in such a short period of time. But he was so much fun and made you feel we had been mates for decades. I think myself and the crew developed early onset lung disease, but it was worth it. He kept in contact for a while by text, helping provide me with mobile numbers for players I couldn't get hold of.

Adam Gilchrist was similar, not in the cigarette department, but in the way he treated me. He was terrific in setting me up with interviews with the likes of Michael Vaughan in England. He would text Vaughan and others, give me a wrap and say I would be in touch so answer the phone. And they did.

I have similar stories for most of the other Australian players. Alan Border was nothing like the Captain Grumpy I had grown up envisaging. He was welcoming and such good company. Ricky Ponting knew a little about me because of his love of AFL footy, so that was handy. His recollection and detail for his career and opponents was an incredible help in crafting the story.

I tried for what seemed like forever to get hold of Merv Hughes but with no luck. I feared Merv. He had left me scarred from an episode many years before. Back when I was a teenager in the country, the Victorian Cricket team used to play some country games with up-and-coming local players. I was around the age of sixteen and selected for one of these games. They split the Victorian team in half and merged us country players into each team. Unfortunately, Merv was on the other team. They showed me the batting order and I was number five or six, I can't quite recall. Back then I was fairly happy with my batting prowess in the local leagues. I was generally a floppy hat wearer, as there were not a lot of tearaways I regularly faced. With the totally unwarranted arrogance of a sixteen-year-old I strutted out to bat like Viv Richards entering the MCG.

Merv, who was bowling at the time, took one look at me and commented, 'Have a look at this bloke will ya…is he fair dinkum? He's wearing a fucking floppy hat; does he have a death wish?'

It went on and on and on. The abuse was staggering. The walk out to the middle felt like it took three and a half hours. I was a mess by the time I asked for middle and leg from the umpire. The local country lads in the field were in a frenzy as well, 'Hit him Merv, knock his fucking head off Merv.'

Hughes was only running in off half his normal run up, but I still didn't see the first ball. It kind of scraped my thigh pad and I hoped like hell it passed the keeper for a leg bye, unfortunately not. I managed to face a few more balls realising he was taking it very easy on me, although that didn't stop the constant barrage of, 'How dare you wear a floppy facing me?' That was my first experience with Merv, and I was still slightly on edge all these years later. When I finally got hold of him his first words were, 'How much coin?' It was a common response from most of the players but coming from Merv it sounded that little more menacing. However, he was unbelievable in the film. He couldn't have been more engaging, and his character and stories shone

191

out like a beacon. But I never found the nerve to revisit the floppy hat episode with him.

Two of the biggest fish I wanted to catch were Dennis Lillee and Jeff Thompson but I only managed to snag 'Thommo.' I had been given his mobile phone number from one of the past players. I won't reveal who other than it was a person who might have had a pretty good TAB set up in his backyard.

I tried Thommo a couple of times with no answer. I texted and left messages with no response. I absolutely loathe the process of trying to contact people to take part in these documentaries. It feels like you are stalking them when you have to keep trying and trying. We were heading up to Queensland to meet and interview some of the players who lived up that way. As Thommo also lived in Queensland it was as good a chance as any to grab him.

When I tried his mobile phone one more time on the day before we were due to fly up there it felt like my last ditch effort.

'Hello,' a voice answered.

'Hi, is this Jeff?' I said.

'Yep, who's this?'

'It's Pete Dickson, mate. I've left a few messages re an Ashes documentary I'd love you to be part of,' I said in the most hopeful tone ever known.

'Oh, yeah, sorry mate I haven't got back to you, been fucking busy. I'm under the fucking car at the minute doing some work on the shit heap.'

Brilliant. At least he wasn't wiping me off yet so there was some hope.

'Are you from Cricket Australia'? he enquired.

'No, I'm not from Cricket Australia but they have commissioned me to make this film.'

'What the fuck does that mean? Is it for Cricket Australia or for you?' he barked.

'Well, it's ultimately for Cricket Australia, yes,' I responded.

'Is there any money involved? If they want me in this fucking thing, they better fucking pay me some money.'

There was not a large purse to pay those taking part, so all I could do was offer the amount we could stretch to for his time.

'Shit that's not much,' was his blunt response.

'Who else has been interviewed for this thing?' he asked.

I ran through the names including the likes of Doug Walters and some of his old team-mates and thought this might tip him over the line. He asked if I had got Dennis Lillee. 'No, unfortunately I can't seem to get hold of him,' I said.

'Yeah, he's fucking hard to get in contact with, he doesn't do much of this type of thing,' he said in a much calmer tone.

There followed a pregnant pause. I didn't know how to approach this and I didn't want to blow the one chance I was having. I told him I was in Queensland the following day and would come to wherever he was to make it as easy as possible for a thirty-minute chat. This was all it would take.

'Well I don't want you to come to my house,' he said.

'No worries we could meet you anywhere easy for you. Name the place and time and we'll be all set up ready to go.'

I was almost pleading but to my great surprise he said okay. I was beyond excited on the other end of the phone, trying to stay cool. He offered a venue which he frequented on the water's edge not far from his home. All good, we agreed I would call him tomorrow to remind him and confirm we were good to go, and he would meet us there.

Flying up to Queensland I was buzzing that Thommo would be taking part. He was and is such an iconic figure in Australian cricket and if I couldn't get Lillee, I had to ensure Thommo would be in the film. The next day myself and my small team did what he requested. We managed to be set up and ready to roll at the exact location he wanted. I rang him as agreed the day before to tell him we were good to go.

'G'day Jeff, it's Pete Dickson we spoke yesterday.'

'Who?' he growled.

'Pete Dickson,' I responded, now a little toey.

'What do you want?' he said. Now I was more than a little toey.

'We spoke yesterday about the Ashes doco, mate. We're here at the place you wanted to meet and ready to go.'

There was another brief pause, it felt he might have changed his mind and was about to fob me off, something that happens more than you would imagine in making documentaries. You never feel confident until interview footage is in the can.

His voice came back down the line. 'Oh fuck, mate, I've just put a DVD movie on,' suggesting he would give the interview a miss and watch the movie instead. It felt like I was speaking to my older brother Graham, who was about the same vintage. He sounded a bit like Graham and had that cheeky, 'I don't give a shit' tone to which I was well accustomed. I decided to speak to him like I would speak to Graham. This would work or fail miserably.

'Thommo, come on mate, get off the couch and get your arse down here, we're ready to go. I have an ice-cold pint waiting for you as well. I need you, mate. It won't be an Ashes film without you involved so forget the DVD for an hour or so.'

I heard a kind of chortle; my gambit might have worked.

'What do I need to wear?' he said.

'Whatever you want mate, very casual,' I said.

'All I have are fucking Hawaiian shirts, I'll wear one of them.'

'Perfect,' I said and he hung up. Phew.

About five minutes later he rang back. I saw his name on the phone and looked at my camera ops, Lincoln and Justin, with an expression of 'oh no.'

'Jeff,' I answered.

'Yeah, what do you want now you just rang?'

'No mate, I didn't ring, we spoke five minutes ago.'

'I've just got a fucking missed call from you,' he said.

This was going well I thought. He must have looked at his phone and seen one of my previously missed calls from the day before. I thought of Graham again.

'Mate, I didn't call you, we're here waiting, are you on your way?'

'Yeah five minutes away, don't know what the fuck is going on with my phone.' His voice trailed out as the phone disconnected.

Ten minutes later the great man entered the building, resplendent with long flowing grey hair and bright Hawaiian shirt and everything I had imagined him to be, a specimen of a man. I walked over to introduce myself and he gave me a strong handshake. His demeanour was warm and not what I expected at all.

'You did fucking call me, you know that don't you,' he said with a smile as he sat down.

'Show me your phone and I'll show you mine,' I responded. 'I absolutely didn't call you, you're making that up.'

He roared with laughter and said I was full of shit but let's get on with it. One of the boys had got him a cold pint so he could have a sip as we went if he wanted to. He demanded I have one as well. So here we were, sitting on a balcony by the ocean, having a few beers and recording. He was simply fantastic and happily chatted for nearly two hours. Nothing was out of bounds, he just let loose.

One of the best and most enjoyable encounters I've ever had in documentary filmmaking took place that day. After all the effort and stalking by me, we finally had Thommo in the can. As he left, he thanked us and said he had had a good time. His final words as he departed were, 'Hey, good luck with all this, I hope you nail it.'

CHAPTER 27

ON THE COUCH

It was now late May 2017 and I had just landed at Heathrow Airport, London. Unfortunately, I didn't have a sleeping pill like the one I was given years earlier on the long flight home from South Africa so arrived in London without any sleep and extremely jet-lagged. I had been to England a few times before but there was a very different atmosphere this time around. During my flight there had been a terror attack at the Manchester Arena. The UK population were scared and on edge. I had arrived to interview the English contingent to complete the remaining part of the documentary. Living in Melbourne, Australia, I hadn't been exposed to the fear of imminent terror attacks in my home city. Stepping foot in London, you could feel the tension and fear wherever you went.

We were staying at the Danubius Hotel in Regents Park, directly opposite the Lord's Cricket Ground. Shane Warne had told me before I left how he used to stay there at times with the

Australian cricket team. Fair to say he wasn't a huge wrap for the place, but it was perfectly situated for what we needed to do. It was ideal for the interviews as many of the English players often flowed through Lord's.

The stress I felt on this trip was unlike anything I had experienced in documentary filmmaking. I really didn't feel safe in London. Instead of enjoying being there, I was already looking forward to getting back on the plane and returning to Australia. We were on a tight schedule due to being in the country for only two weeks. The uncertainty of whether some of the planned interviews would go ahead, or whether players had changed their minds was constant. I got very lucky at times. Over dinner one night at a pub next to Lords, I noticed Angus Fraser. I had emailed him a few times from Australia with no response. I'm sure he must have thought I was stalking him when I approached him at the pub. But he was so obliging and locked in an interview for the very next day. Just lucky.

A similar thing happened with Alec Stewart. I was having breakfast at the 'Royal Danubius' as we started calling it, when Alec walked in for breakfast. He happened to be staying at the same place. Again, I took the chance to harass him over his bacon and eggs and he was more than happy to take part.

I found the English players, past and present, had a really refreshing attitude towards the general population. They didn't seem to have many qualms about mingling with Joe Public. They went about their business as normal people without much ego or 'look at me' type of behaviour. I found them wonderful company. Maybe I just got lucky with the players I was interviewing, and they are totally different from others in England, but it was very evident to me.

I had met John Emburey, or 'Embers,' an English cricket legend through Bruce Eva. He was instrumental in helping me line up players while there. Such a gentleman. On our final night in London, he hosted us at his home for dinner with his family. This was incredibly kind and spoke volumes about the man. However, camera operator Lincoln and I had to hide our reactions to Embers supplying us with Foster's beer ... it's funny that the English still think we actually drink Foster's in Australia.

Andrew Strauss was one of the nicest human beings I have come across. Time spent with Michael Vaughan (thanks to Gilly) at his local cricket ground was priceless. The staff at Lord's Cricket Ground were unbelievably helpful. We were given tremendous access at Lord's for any filming we needed. Being up close with the original Ashes urn and all the history within the place is astounding. It was a phenomenal experience. Alastair Cook and Jonny Bairstow gave me a few hours of their time chatting in the Lord's library. David 'Bumble' Lloyd was the English version of Thommo. Such fun and full of character, he added so much to the film.

It was a whirlwind, stressful and incredible adventure all rolled into one. Two days before I was to fly home there was another terror attack with stabbings on London Bridge. I had been to this very area only a few days before. As I strapped myself into my Qantas seat, I could not have been happier to be flying home to Australia.

'Hi Pete, it's Sue.'

I had just unpacked my bags back at home and although tired and a little grumpy from the long flight, I was glad to hear my sister's voice on the phone.

'Hey Sis, how are you?' I said before hearing her burst into tears. She was phoning to tell me that mum was dying and probably only had a few days to live.

I nearly dropped the phone. Mum had been battling dementia for some years. She was now living in an elderly care facility in Morwell. Ever since Rob's death I felt mum had lost her zest for life. Her heartbreak seemed to consume her and she slowly but surely deteriorated. When visiting her, it was hard to establish if she recognised you or was just being polite. She wasn't in great shape when I left for England, but this news was nonetheless very sudden, she had gone downhill so quickly while I was away.

Sue and my brothers had not wanted to tell me while I was in England. They didn't want to add that to my worries. I was really annoyed at them for not telling me. Thankfully, mum hadn't died before I got home so I rushed straight to her bedside. Sue had done an amazing effort supporting mum over the years. Sue lived locally and was the one who really took over the care of her. A few days later mum passed. It felt like another kick of grief in the guts for the family. But it was a different grief. She hadn't been well for a very long time and, if anything, there was a feeling of relief that her agony was over. It was a different pain from what we had with Rob and the boys. This was sad because we had lost our mum. The woman who gave birth and raised us. She was hard work at times, but she loved us with all her heart and only ever wanted the best for her children. I would miss her deeply. For me it added another layer on top of what I was still going through with Rob. She once said to me after Rob's death how she had wanted to die so she could be with him again. I was hoping her wish was now somehow being fulfilled.

Following the funeral, I had to get back to work as time was running out to complete the film. I was almost living in the edit suite. My team of Mel and Che, who is my long-time freelance editor, were also working feverishly around the clock.

It was a Monday night in early August when it all came crashing down for me. I had woken in the early hours shaking uncontrollably. I was in the midst of a nervous breakdown. My wife was petrified and I felt like I had let her down. It was so embarrassing to be in this situation. Having to see a psychiatrist was not something I was proud of or ever expected in my wildest dreams. I felt weak. I had always believed from a young age that I was as solid as a rock, this was what my mother had told me my name meant. I took it to heart. Living through kidney problems, Rob's tragedy, I thought I had handled most things well. I was solid, strong. But now here I was, being told by Dr Chris Walsh I would be dead within twelve months if I didn't get help and treatment.

I had avoided therapists and their ilk like the plague since Rob's death. I was convinced it wasn't for me. But now sitting on this couch I knew I was in deep trouble. In my first few sessions with Dr Walsh I let everything flood out. I hadn't spoken like this to anyone, ever. He sat and listened and listened and listened.

What was wrong with me? I wanted a quick answer, some medication and to get on with life again. All good. Let's go, doc. But I soon learnt it was not going to be this easy. There were many things I was struggling with according to him, but the overriding issue he first wanted to deal with was my grief surrounding Rob's death. He pinned this straight away as something which I hadn't fully dealt with. Part of me instantly felt his observation was bullshit. It's been eight years, I'm fine. But when he looked me directly in the eye after saying Rob's name, I burst into uncontrollable tears. It had all finally caught up with me.

This was an awakening in the sense of accepting I needed help. I was lucky the warning signs manifested to the extent of full body shaking and shutdown, instead of something worse. I soon became a regular on the couch as I began treatment and started the long road to trying to get better.

I had a responsibility to finish *Forged in Fire*. I had to keep working on the film. There was no option to take a spell at that stage. So I went back into the edit suite and the bubble of crafting the doco. Two months later I was showing Ben and Richard the drafts.

My main concern was that Cricket Australia would want to censor the language. What I was most proud of was how open and expressive all the players were in the interviews. They didn't hold back, and this included the use of fruity language.

Normally, when previously seen on television, it was all very fluffy and straight down the line; the standard boring stuff being repeated over and over again.

But this doco was raw, it was unfiltered and for me it felt real. To its credit, CA agreed and let it run as intended. No doubt this was risky. But I was delighted it took the chance. I have always been so invested and passionate about the work I take on, so it meant there were times when I had battles with Cricket Australia on various creative elements, but in the end we got there.

Cricket Australia organised a big launch in Brisbane during the first Ashes Test of the summer. I had to speak on a panel at an event hosted by Mark Nicholas which included Greg Chappell and Graeme Swann. There was a lot of press and much hype about the documentary series, and I had to do the rounds of promotion. This included the RSN radio interview on Daniel Harford's breakfast show. This was the interview in which I thought I my legitimacy as a filmmaker was being questioned. Leaving the studio that day my insecurities took over again. I should have been out there promoting and being confident in celebrating this soon to be released TV series, yet here I was consumed with negative thoughts and self-doubt.

When I look back I feel I really didn't give myself a chance to enjoy any of what was happening. I know my mental state had been deteriorating but I was so manic about making this film a masterpiece. It was the film of my life at the time. This was my chance to break out of Rob's shadow and make something in a code other than football. Even though I had delivered what would go on to be a critically acclaimed and award-winning documentary, I still felt like a fraud. A poor man's Rob Dickson.

When I read these words now, I see madness in thinking this way. Totally wasted energy to even bother with such thoughts. It simply didn't matter. No one gave a shit about any of it. Most people who watch these films don't even register who made them. So just be who you are and be happy with that. But I couldn't control it, I so badly wanted to be his equal. This whole chase to be like Rob, suddenly materialised into the pointless pursuit it really was. You will rarely, if ever, change someone's opinion of you if they are against you — so let it go.

CHAPTER 28

TWO NATIONS, ONE OBSESSION

In the months following the release of *Forged in Fire* I retreated into another solid reclusive state of living. It was somewhat of a pattern for me following big projects to need a re-charge, but this was different. I was now aware of the work I needed to do on myself. I was seeing Dr Walsh regularly. Thankfully, I started to sleep a little better, or more to the point, sleep at all. It was an interesting time. I felt I was breaking through a kind of mist that had constantly hung inches in front of me for years. I started to be a little more rational in my thinking and less emotional about everything. Thank goodness.

An example of how well I was travelling only months beforehand was when I took the kids to see the movie Sing. They still rag me to this day about the fact I was crying at the end of the movie. I remember them staring at me wondering why I was tearing up and they weren't. It's a kid's movie! It got to me though, pathetic stuff from a grown adult, but this is how on the edge I was emotionally. I still refuse to watch Sing 2 at any stage.

Cricket Australia got in touch to let me know it was keen to make another film. This time it would be based around the India v Australia rivalry and history. *Forged in Fire* had done well and was now seemingly everywhere on DVD as well. I'm certain my dad ensured they would have to print a second run of Forged *in Fire* DVDs. He drained most stores of stock by purchasing as many as he could. He would send them to every family member and friend he knew. It then moved on to friends of friends and strangers in the street he might have accidentally bumped into. He was proud as punch, and I loved that it made him happy.

In a perfect world I would have spent much more time trying to get healthy and not jump straight back into another big feature. But when opportunities such as this present themselves, you cannot dismiss them. Who knew when the next major project would come knocking on my door? After working through a new contract with Cricket Australia, I agreed to terms to make a second film which would be called *2 Nations, 1 Obsession*.

I was soon immersed in its production. This film would have a completely different feel to *Forged in Fire*. This was much more of a story about a battle of cultures in my eyes. Most of those I approached this time were keen to be involved, mainly because of knowing more about me thanks to the success of *Forged in Fire*. One of the most common questions I get following the release of a documentary is, 'Why didn't you interview so and so for this film?' In nearly every case the person they are talking about was asked to take part but declined. 'I tried,' is my common response to those asking.

In a perfect world you would have large budgets that would make it hard for the talent to say no if you could pay what they wanted, but it's not a perfect world. The most common reason for people declining to take part is that they generally want more money than is available. There are others reticent to be involved for different reasons. I remember Matthew Hayden saying he didn't feel we were aligned from a content perspective. I hadn't even started creating the film so am still not sure what he meant by that ... but I tried, that's all you can do.

Travelling to India for the first time was a shock to the senses. I thought I was prepared after hearing so many stories about the place. But it was still a massive jolt to the system. The heat, the smells, the sheer weight of the population, the noise. It was all-consuming. We arrived in Mumbai for two weeks of frantically trying to line up past and present Indian players. This was incredibly difficult. As most cricketing followers know the Indian players are revered as gods in their home country. They cannot walk outside without being mobbed. How different compared to the English players who I had witnessed mingling with the public with ease.

We managed to entice the likes of Kapil Dev, Sunil Gavaskar, Ravi Shastri, and several others to take part including Harsha Bhogle. So even though it was challenging and a constant source of panic in securing the interviews, we made it happen. Ravi Shastri was the highlight for me. He gave me a call back after I had tried several times. He was the current coach of India at that stage. His demeanour and manner were smooth and full of positive energy. After the normal introductions he got straight to the point and wanted to know, 'How many dollars Pete?' Regardless of nationality, many things remain the same.

Ravi was such a fascinating and engaging man. He provided so much content for the film with his charm and cheeky nature. He even gracefully accepted cameraman Lincoln suddenly departing the shoot and running out the door looking for the nearest toilet. Linc had bragged the night before of how much street food he had consumed. Might have even called me soft for not having a crack myself at the local cuisine out on the boardwalk. This was the result of his culinary exploits. He spent the next twenty-four hours hanging on to the toilet, both ends causing chaos. Ravi took it in his stride, 'Not the first Australian, and certainly won't be the last Australian I witness struggling with our street food,' he roared with laughter.

The staff at the hotel where we held most of the interviews were beside themselves when these greats of the game entered the building for interviews. It was mayhem. I really have no idea how the players live in such an environment. But they seem to take it all in their stride, hero worshipped to the absolute extreme. I had never seen anything remotely like it. The people of India were lovely, friendly, and polite. We flew out of Mumbai exhausted but feeling satisfied we had gathered just what we needed for the film.

By this stage deep into production I was starting to wane again. I knew I was in a much better place mentally than a year ago, but I could still feel myself slipping. Thus it was more relief than excitement for me once we had finished the film. It was released on the Fox Sports network before the Australia v India series, held in Australia.

2 Nations, 1 Obsession remains one of my proudest achievements. It was a completely different looking documentary from *Forged in Fire*, much more alive in a cultural sense thanks to the unique country and people of India. It was my last production for Cricket Australia. After two very intense years working together, we were done. I'm forever grateful to Richard and Ben for giving me that opportunity to create two feature documentaries for a sport I loved. This experience, although right in the midst of my own personal battles, was life changing for me. I know they are very proud to have those two films in the Cricket Australia productions catalogue.

CHAPTER 29

SPUD

Following such an intense and frantic two years spent developing the cricket films, we took another detour in subject matter for our next few projects. We were approached to tell the story of the legendary Australian racehorse Winx and her epic Cox Plate victories. To be given the chance to document on film one of the greatest achievements in racing history, was a huge thrill, and something I cherished.

I was still very focussed on my health, trying to balance my working life with recovery. I had started to believe, rather than try to convince myself, that I was doing okay in the filmmaking space. More than okay. This was a big change of thought process for me. The incredible support and help from my doctor and those close to me was starting to bear fruit. I was letting go of some of that baggage I was dragging around. I had begun to realise the constant desire to reach a mythical level of Rob in my head was simply unhealthy. That manic chase became less important. The focus had shifted to the main issue of trying to deal with the loss of Rob. It sounds ridiculous after so many years, but this was, and is, the real battle raging in my head behind everything else.

The grief began to manifest itself in odd ways. I started dreaming of him constantly. Over the years I would have the occasional dream about Rob that was more like a horror movie. Now I was dreaming more about enjoyable times with Rob front and centre. I accepted being sad about things such as my kids not having their Uncle Rob in their lives. Sad about not having their gorgeous cousins, Gabe and Byron, to grow up with. Previously, I was not aware I was refusing to let myself even think about these things. Ignored them as much as I could.

Now I had begun to accept them and to let myself process it as real, let myself be sad. It's not easy. Showing my kids the series of Rob's *Survivor* season was incredibly cathartic for me. It sounds strange but it was. To be able to witness my children seeing their uncle right there on screen, with all his humour and personality, was priceless. Thanks to a TV series they got to know their uncle and understand why I loved and missed him so much. To hear them say his voice was just like mine, or his facial expressions were just like mine, so many similarities they would never have known if not for this *Survivor* season. We are all so very grateful we have this to look back on.

It was now September 2019. Our second racing documentary *Winx IV* was about to be released on Channel Seven and Racing. com. I was looking forward to a holiday in Japan with my family.

We were days away from flying out when the news broke that Danny 'Spud' Frawley had died.

This was a hammer blow of the highest order. I loved Spud and his wife Anita so very much. He was such a large presence in my life. I had known him well and enjoyed his company before Rob died, but he went to another level for me following Rob's tragedy. He wrapped his arms around me and was a constant figure in my life. He often checked in on me and we worked together on many projects. Only months before, he and Anita were at my house celebrating my birthday and he looked as happy as I had seen him in years. I have a photo of him and Anita from that night that I treasure. But this put me right back into a bad place. I was so utterly sick and tired of feeling sad. Anita gave me a call and she was broken. She asked if I could help with the funeral by making a video tribute for Danny.

'Of course, whatever you need,' I told her.

It was the very least I could do to help.

Ness and the kids flew out to Japan and I stayed home, delaying my trip until after the funeral. I went around to Anita's house and spent a few hours with her and the girls. My heart was in pieces for her and Danny's beautiful daughters. They wanted to put their own tributes to Danny on the video presentation instead of speaking at the funeral. We all sat in Anita's living room, camera rolling. Without question I've never had to film anything so gut-wrenching. Sitting there listening to them pour out their deep love for Danny and the intense pain at him being no longer in their life, was something I will never forget.

I left their home some hours later and cried all the way home. I was right back where I was with Rob years earlier. Danny wasn't my brother, so it had a different effect on me, it was more a sick feeling of hurt for Anita and the girls. I knew what they were enduring.

I spent the next few days before the funeral in an edit-suite putting together the tribute video of Danny. It felt like deja-vu. At times I felt like I was editing my own pain with Rob and the boys into what I was making, I kept having to check myself to take my own emotions out of what I was putting together. It was incredibly difficult. All I could hope was that I had done justice to Danny. The trust that Anita and the girls placed in me to get this right on their behalf was enormous, so I couldn't let them down. That loomed large over me. Without much sleep and totally wrung out, I attended Danny's funeral. I couldn't even gather energy to speak to people. I hid up the back in the standing room. The funeral was so well done by all involved. At the end, the video tribute was introduced as a closer to the service. Before it started to play, I left the building. After crafting it and seeing the devastation in his family for days on end while editing, I couldn't even look at it one more time. I found myself in a bad place again mentally. I went home and sat in my lounge room alone with my thoughts, probably not the best thing to be doing. I needed my family.

The next day I flew to Japan to join up with them. This trip proved to be perfect timing. Arriving and having Luke, Abby, and Sasha sprint to me for hugs was like taking a breath of fresh air. Being with my wife and kids, travelling around Japan was just what I needed. I will never forget Danny and what he meant to Rob and me.

Without warning, the world descended into chaos a few months later. Covid-19 was sweeping the globe. Like everyone else, we were holed up in our homes and unable to work for the majority of 2020. As an obstetrician, my wife Ness is classified as an essential worker, so was able to continue her daily routine. I remained home with the three children who were now home-schooling. I found this time very therapeutic. It enabled a certain kind of inner peace such as I hadn't experienced for a long while. Other than the odd day of cabin fever, I didn't mind those first few months locked away from the world.

Deep in lockdown and without any certainty of what lay ahead, I received a call from Brent Williams, the director of sport at Channel Nine. He wanted to know if I was keen to make a documentary covering all the major sporting codes that were stuck in a Covid bubble at the time in Queensland. Obviously, I was locked down in Melbourne so that would be difficult. But they were more than happy for me to produce and direct from home, conducting most of the interviews via zoom. The turnaround was fast. With some of my team working on the ground in Queensland we had to complete this film in world record time for us. This tested any filmmaking skills I may or may not have to the extreme. Interviewing over zoom, crafting stories of a range of sporting codes into one film, dealing with the restrictions and the limitations that Covid presented in filming and gathering of footage, was challenging to say the least.

All the heads of major sporting codes including AFL, rugby

league, V8 supercars, netball, boxing willingly took part. It was a joy to include Gillon McLachlan as the CEO of the AFL and spend time with him again for the film, albeit over zoom.

The Sporting Bubble was released on Channel Nine during November 2020. To end up with such a high-quality television documentary in such circumstances, was an extraordinary achievement from my team. I am very proud of them and the film as it captured a hugely significant moment in time for our sporting codes amidst the pandemic.

As the lockdown continued on and on and on in Melbourne and we wondered if we would ever be able to leave the house again, I was speaking over the phone regularly with Nathan Lovett-Murray. Nathan is an ex-AFL player with Essendon now working with the St Kilda Football Club, as its Indigenous liaison officer. Nathan had created a program called Point + Be Proud. It was a school program to educate young people about the impacts of racism on our mental health.

His inspiration for the program was Nicky Winmar and the iconic photo taken in 1993 by photographer Wayne Ludbey at Victoria Park, Collingwood. Nicky had been racially abused by a rabid Collingwood supporter base and at the end of the game lifted his jumper to point at his Black skin. He was showing them how proud he was to be a Black man. Nathan, a proud Indigenous man himself, has a relentless passion to make real change in community behaviours and attitudes. So, the early seeds of a possible documentary were being discussed. The problem, even during the best of times economically, let alone during a worldwide pandemic, is in funding such projects. I therefore doubted he would be able to secure funding to enable us to proceed with production. Then late in 2020 I received a call from Nathan.

'Pete, it's Nat.'

'Hi mate, how's things?' I said.

'Amazing, I have secured funding for the documentary.'

I was stunned. How the hell did he pull that off? He had managed to get funding approved from VicHealth, which was an incredible result. His tenacious and relentless drive to make this happen had paid off. All credit to him. Within a few weeks production was under way on my most important film to date, *The Ripple Effect*.

CHAPTER 30

THE RIPPLE EFFECT

Kurt Fearnley was up on stage at the Sport Australia Media Awards in Sydney in March 2022. He was there as a special guest to announce the winner of the documentary award for Best Depiction of Inclusive Sport. It was a surreal moment for me as I had long admired this champion Paralympic gold medallist. The room was silent as he announced, 'The winner is Peter Dickson, *The Ripple Effect*.' I was sitting at a table alongside my wife Ness, Nathan Lovett-Murray, and my team including Jo Stuckey and Mel Mullen. I couldn't believe it. Our little film had won this most prestigious award. It was a triumph for Nathan's dogged determination and will to make it happen.

From the moment Nathan first called me to discuss the possibility of taking this film on, I was reticent to say the least. All I could think was how can someone close to being the whitest person in Australia, tell this Indigenous story of racism and its debilitating effects on mental health in this country. This was my fear and I mentioned to Nathan how it was probably best to be put in the hands of an Indigenous director. But he was relentless and adamant he wanted me to make this film. A few years earlier I had worked closely with his family on a smaller film about his legendary great-grandfather, Pastor Sir Doug Nicholls. Nathan apparently felt there was a connection there and he kept persisting. The budget in terms of a feature documentary, compared to others of a similar ilk, was very modest. Coming out of a sustained period of lockdown and Covid, it was still somewhat of a surprise any money was available at all, so we took it on and did the best we could with the resources we had.

I had met Nicky Winmar a couple of times back in the day through Rob and he is great company. The burden and weight he's carried since making his stance so many years ago still lives within. He gave us his heart and opened his soul for this film. This became more than making a documentary for me. It affected me to the core. Interviewing the likes of Nova Peris, Nathan, professional surfer Otis Carey, Bachar Houli, Akec Makur Chuot and Josh Addo-Carr to name a few, was at times harrowing. Listening to their own deeply personal experiences suffering racism was nothing like I had experienced when interviewing. The ongoing damage to people's lives and mental health is real and heartbreaking. I often felt sick to my stomach during the production. The bullying, the abuse, the sheer lack of respect they had experienced all their lives, even to this day, made me shudder. The responsibility to tell this story properly on their behalf, and make it have a long-lasting impact, weighed heavily on me. Nathan's guidance and support throughout was crucial. Separate from the feature length documentary we also produced a fifteen-minute version, which Nathan now uses as part of his Point + Be Proud school educational program. We are incredibly proud of that.

I had hoped that a network would pick it up as I believe every Australian needs to see this film. Thankfully, it was taken by Channel Seven even though this was not a subject that sat comfortably in its preferred broadcast schedule. Documentaries of this nature were more likely to appear on SBS or the ABC. But with the AFL element and Nicky Winmar's story being the thread, it found a place. Unfortunately, it was slotted to go to air following a night game, which meant it didn't get a start until well after 11 pm. Not ideal in any sense. Those sorts of time slots grate on me but what can you do, it's out of your control. Thankfully SBS and NITV also took an option to broadcast the film and did so in March 2022. The time slot was a Sunday night, prime time 8.30 pm.

Without question *The Ripple Effect* production was the most important and meaningful piece of work I have been involved with. The pain and trauma racism in this country inflicts on our Indigenous population daily is disgusting, and seemingly never ending. The hope which emerges from the film is it will cease through generational change. Out of all the films I have made to date, this is the one that I hope has some kind of influence on changing behaviours. Even if it's only a small influence, it is something.

NAME **ROBERT**, 38, film/video producer. Married with one child. BORN and currently lives in Victoria. DESCRIBES HIMSELF AS positive, persistent and ambitious.

Australian Survivor series promotion

Beard in the wild: Rob during filming of the Survivor series

Champion: moments after being announced winner of Australian Survivor

*With Rob at the Survivor
finale afterparty*

An all-time favourite photo: with my brothers at Ricky's wedding

*Perfect pairing: Rob was
always happy when on the
beach and with his camera*

In the thick of it: Rob doing his thing in among players celebrating the 2008 Premiership

Great mates: Rob with Shane Crawford on the MCG after the 2008 Grand Final

Man at work: Rob in the edit suite wearing his typical daily attire

Do Not Disturb: Rob deep in editing mode for
The Essence of the Game film

The Essence of the Game DVD sleeve

Legacy of a life cut sadly short

THE BUZZ

JON RALPH

ROBERT Dickson's life was filled with so many extraordinary feats it was scarcely believable.

Hawthorn footballer, international missionary, Australian *Survivor* winner and AFL football's greatest documentary-maker — it was a life packed with action.

His brother Peter even has in his mind the opening scene of the documentary he would one day like to create about a life cut short.

Monday marked the seventh anniversary of the death of Robert and his two sons Gabriel, 8, and Byron, 5, in a South African car accident.

From an early age, Dickson was different.

Australia's youngest helicopter pilot at 17, he re-created one of cinema's great moments.

It was at the Traralgon Drive-In, where Dickson was timing his moment as Wagner's *Ride Of The Valkyries* blared out over the speakers.

"He was shocking in a helicopter, he just bent the rules everywhere, flying everywhere and going to pick up his girlfriend from a farm," Peter Dickson recalled this week.

"One day they were sitting there watching *Apocalypse Now* and he timed it with that famous scene where the helicopters fly over.

"He hovered behind the drive-in screen and as the scene came on he lifted up across the top of the screen and the place went crazy.

"It was like it was in 3D."

That documentary is on the backburner — Robert Dickson's death is still too raw — but his filmmaking has lived on through his brother's work.

For seven years he has created the breathtaking short films for the AFL's season launches and a series of stunning documentaries on famous AFL Grand Finals and the league's captains and coaches.

Now he is breaking away from the AFL in a move that will also bring to life his brother's filmmaking legacy. He has formed the independent Dickson Films, with his new website (dicksonfilms.com.au) a treasure trove of his brother's AFL documentaries.

The brothers were budding filmmakers pushing the boundaries together when Robert was killed, but he likes the synergy of completing seven of the AFL's season launch films — the same number as Robert, who was an emergency in the famed 1989 Grand Final.

And if this year's effort is his last, capturing Cyril Rioli returning home from Grand Final heroics for a traditional indigenous dance with his father would be hard to top.

Dickson, who will work a day a week with the AFL while exploring outside projects, said he has never gotten over his brother's death.

"I don't think I handled the grief all that well because I still don't think I have shaken it," he said. "My kids are my joy, but what happens is you don't have that spontaneous joy.

"I used to have joy. It is all traced back to (his accident) and it's hard to get too excited about things, which is s--t.

"It just sucks. He was my big brother and my hero and he was so good-looking and talented and funny.

"I haven't laughed at all like I used to laugh with him."

He said publicly releasing his brother's work was fitting given he feels like Robert has guided his own filmmaking.

The synergies are perfect: Robert's 2008 Grand Final film captured Alastair Clarkson demanding his players "Kill the shark". Last year Peter grabbed Clarkson's pregame theme "Time to Hunt".

jon.ralph@news.com.au
@RalphyHeraldSun

See previously unseen Dickson Films vision
heraldsun.com.au

Former Hawthorn footballer and film maker, the late Robert Dickson.

As the press saw it: a report of Rob's death and his filmmaking legacy

Me with Graham, Sue, dad and Ricky at the cemetery

Remembering Rob: now only five of us

A loss long ago

I was only very small and young,
when the sad news bounced off my ~~tounge~~ tongue.
The news that left my Dad in pain,
the special people that do not remain.
I was too young to understand,
I wish they were still standing on this land.
The people who said they would have been fun,
to the sad thought of saying goodbye.

Not knowing much about them at all,
I'm not running off to have a ball.
The news that breaks anyones heart,
them and I are now apart.
The pain of seeing his pale face,
is harder than a running race.
I don't remember anything,
the photo's tell me everything.

The vehicle that was driven around,
that has a quiet engine sound,
Is the reason for this tragedy,
No one will get through it casually.
A tragedy that no man can solve,
but if you still have to stay brave,
he's famous till today,
you'll see him in a photo one day.

The end has to come with everyone,
some grandparents have said goodbye to their grandson.
It could be young or old,
but it breaks a spirit in your heart thats cold.
Everyone faces a sad goodbye,
The same as I.

Precious words: the poem written by my daughter Abby

Out with the crew filming for The Chosen Few series

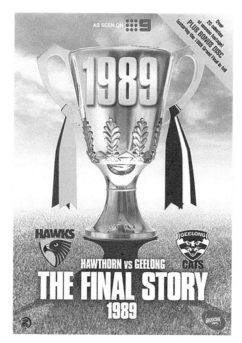

The Final Story 1989 DVD sleeve

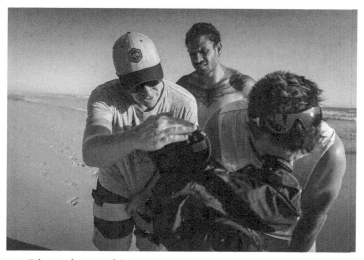

Filming for one of the AFL season launch films with Cyril Rioli

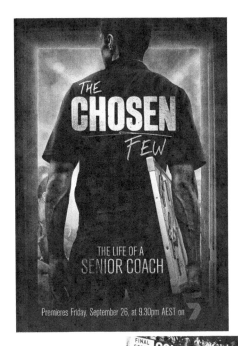

Premiere: The
Chosen Few poster

The Final Draw
documentary

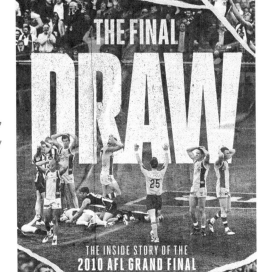

Family: here with mum and my children
Abby, Sasha and Luke

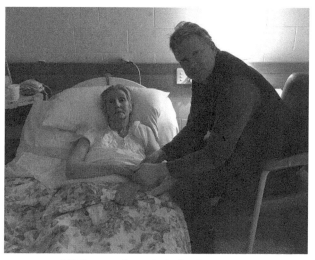

With mum the night before her passing

Don and Sue with mum during her last few months

All together: my large and much loved extended family after mum's funeral

Talking to Thommo: interviewing Jeff Thompson for the Forged in Fire documentary

Interviewing Shane Warne for the Forged in Fire documentary

*Launching Cricket Australia's Forged in Fire: Mark Nicholas,
me, Greg Chappell and Graeme Swann*

*DVD sleeves: 2
Nations, 1 Obsession
and Forged in Fire*

The Ripple Effect documentary featuring Nicky Winmar

Sport Australia award for
The Ripple Effect .

Winner 2021 Media Awards

Celebrating with the team: Mel, Jo and Nathan Lovett-Murray

The author with
Gillon MacLachlan

With Anita and Danny 'Spud' Frawley

My brother Rob: how I like to remember him

CHAPTER 31

THE PROFESSION

Following the release of *The Ripple Effect* I have been taking time to reflect on what the future might hold for me in documentary filmmaking. I have become very selective about what I will take on. My priority is not to slide back into unhealthy habits and manic behaviours in trying to reach some unrealistic level of filmmaking. I have also reached a place where if I feel like I have done that, then it's probably not for me. It needs to light my fire and get me passionate about wanting to be involved. If I don't take that passion and energy into the task, then it's futile.

There are many things which must go very right to enable a feature documentary to even start production. First and foremost is the ability to fund the process. This is getting more and more difficult as each year passes. I still field calls weekly with great ideas and concepts. At least two calls a week on average. None though have any means or ability to fund these ideas. So, it becomes pointless even to start these conversations. I have often fallen into the trap of being dragged along an endless road chasing funds that ends up going nowhere. Hundreds of wasted hours earning nothing for your time.

I don't take that route anymore. If someone wants me to make a film, they need to be able to fund it before I begin to consider it. When you work for yourself and rely purely on yourself to earn income, it's brutally difficult to sustain decent earnings. Yes, you might pick up a well-funded project which will enable you to earn sufficiently during the production, but once the film is completed, the earnings stop. You often go many months before another opportunity arises, if at all.

You must be in the game because you have a passion and love for storytelling. This needs to be the motivation. For budding documentary filmmakers out there, if money is what drives you, I strongly urge you to think about something else as an occupation. I have been plain lucky, incredibly lucky. But for a windfall many years ago, and a wife who earns very well in her own profession, I simply could not make these films. Not a chance. Many people would be staggered by how little Rob and I earned over the years in this business. Both of us have unfortunately had what can only be described as a detrimental approach to actually making money. Our focus has always been to pour most of the budgets into the actual production. The overriding goal has been to make the best possible film we can. If this means tipping every cent into making that happen, then so be it. This is wonderful for the film but leaves very little after all is said and done. Quality and emotional impact were a mantra we repeated often to each other. No wonder we failed miserably as business operators when in partnership together.

It's not all doom and gloom, by any means. It has been our choice to work for ourselves. There are many opportunities out there to work for production houses and studios which remove you from the perils of running your own race.

Regardless of whether you work for someone or for yourself, if you are lucky enough to experience the ride of making documentary films you will never regret it. It's so rewarding to see what you have created being viewed and enjoyed by people. No matter whether on the big screen at a cinema, on your TV at home or even on a simple laptop, your work is being watched. This is something I still get a thrill out of to this day. Between us we have now made more than twenty feature sporting documentaries. All of which have found a home on broadcast or pay television. This is somewhat unique I imagine for two brothers, and something of which Rob would have been very proud.

The life experiences and number of fascinating people I have met over all these years working in this profession, is simply priceless. The many people who have worked directly with Rob and I over so long also deserve many plaudits. Not only for putting up with us but for your friendship, advice, assistance, unwavering support and love. Even though he is no longer here I can say this with absolute certainty on his behalf, that we have truly appreciated every one of you. I hope for me these relationships will continue for many years to come.

CHAPTER 32

FILMMAKER OR DUD?

I had just plonked myself on to what looked like a new couch in the rooms of Dr Chris Walsh. 'Have some new trendy furniture I see,' I said with a smile. I've lost count of how many appointments I've had with Chris since that first session back in 2017.

I hadn't seen him face to face in many months because of Covid restrictions. Like everyone else we had been using Zoom for our appointments. As is his wont, he looked at me for a few minutes, evaluating how I appeared. It was comforting to hear him say how well he thought I looked. Compared to the shell of a human being he first laid eyes on a few years earlier I had made some headway. I had come to really look forward to my sessions with Chris. After many years of denial and convincing myself I didn't need help or to talk to anyone about my grief, here I was, a convert.

'Are you writing a book?' he said with his usual positivity.

'Yes, I've been wanting to do something around Rob and our story for a long time now, but I've moved from thoughts about a documentary to writing it down in a book.'

He was delighted. His view was this would do wonders for me in my ongoing battles with grief and dealing with Rob's loss. He was right. Again. This process of writing about my brother has allowed me to celebrate what he's meant to me. I've cried and laughed and reflected and enjoyed the process immensely. By no means do I feel completely healed from the pain of losing Rob. I will never get over it. But I believe I have at least come to terms with it.

You live and learn but I often lament that I didn't seek help much earlier following his passing. Such a stubborn idiot. Everyone has the right to deal with their own grief as they see fit, and in their own way. There is no right or wrong, but if you are struggling to cope, seek help, talk to someone. It was the absolute last thing I wanted to do, until it was forced upon me.

I was reticent because I thought it would be uncomfortable and confronting. It was, but that's the point. It allows you to explore and confront those issues head on, instead of keeping them buried below the surface. The sadness I retain within is a sense of not being happy. I wish I could recapture that emotion of unadulterated happiness in something, in anything. This is a feeling I have struggled to attain since his passing. I've had moments of joy and wonderful experiences with my family but nothing close to what I would describe as pure happiness. Did I ever have it? I believe I did, but maybe deep within there has always been a dark cloud hovering over me. I think of my health concerns as a child and the repercussions from all those issues growing up. Did that seed a level of unhappiness which roared to the surface once tragedy struck? Maybe, but who would ever know?

My wife often picks up on this but is also aware of my ability to put on an act in front of others. I like to think that when I'm around people socially they feel I'm in a good place. The energy it takes to mask what's going on internally is draining at times, but worth it. Who wants to be constantly around someone who is inherently unhappy? No one.

There is no doubt most people who lose a loved one end up eulogising them as much as they possibly can. This is normal and is simply a way of celebrating that person. I definitely eulogised my brother to superhero status, to an untouchable stature.

If you apply any kind of logic to those thoughts, it sounds kind of silly. Rob was Rob. Yes, he was a hero to me, the shining light in my life, but I feel as if I have since placed him at an unrealistic level. He had his issues like everyone else. He wasn't perfect, far from it. So, when I look at it rationally, it does seem a bit over the top. The more I have accepted that fact, the more I have been able to celebrate the role he played in my life, and simply be grateful I had time with him at all.

At times I still drift back into slight depression, often without warning, but I know it won't cripple me and I will soon return to better days. This in itself is a breakthrough. It's a matter of taking it easy on myself and allowing it to happen. I have accepted the ache will always linger inside me, but at least I'm much more aware of what is going on in my own head.

I often think of what Rob would be doing today if still alive. These thoughts then lead me to what I would be doing if Rob was here. I'm certain he would have kept getting better and better at his craft. Would that have taken him towards movies? Possibly. With his personality and screen presence would he have taken on some media roles? Who knows? But I know one thing for certain, if he was passionate about it, then he would have made anything work.

As for me, I would have probably continued under his wing to some degree, firmly entrenched in the knowledge I have a creative back-up in Rob. With him around I doubt I would have had the fortitude and drive to advance my own filmmaking to the level I have. I really don't know what would have happened, who possibly could, but I always felt like the understudy, the bass player to him standing out front singing loud. It feels very far-fetched to think that I alone would have made the films I have over the years if Rob were still here. I cannot see it.

People often say to me that 'Rob would be up there so proud of you with the work you do.' There was a time when I loved to hear this. But the reality is that I know Rob was proud of me anyway. He loved me like he loved his whole family. Of course, he would be proud and happy I continued doing what he loved to do, but if I hadn't, it wouldn't have changed a single thing about how he felt about me.

It's no coincidence that since my breakdown episode I have given up the chase to be like Rob in a filmmaking sense. The relentless pursuit driving me to make film after film to keep his legacy alive was killing me. I have learnt, albeit very slowly, to be comfortable with just being me. It's taken a lot of work to reach this point, and there is still plenty of work I need to do on myself.

But in a filmmaking sense, I'm at a place where I no longer feel the need to achieve that level of excellence I believe Rob had attained. I am who I am, the way I craft storytelling today is my way. Rob introduced me to a style many years ago which held me in good stead. Since then, I have developed my own methods and have a high level of confidence in my own abilities. As each year passes, I am more comfortable that whatever I produce is the best I can do. If not good enough for some, then so be it. But for those who do enjoy my work I'm so grateful and thankful to each of them for watching.

When I think back on my self-doubt about the question of being an actual documentary filmmaker, or a complete dud, I wish I had never allowed myself to even consider those thoughts. It's so damaging. Unfortunately, I did consider this question constantly and I cannot take the time back. My view on how I perceive myself now is very different to back then. Who cares?... is what I think. No one. Call yourself what you like. Just be comfortable with who you are. If I am a poor man's Rob Dickson, then brilliant. What an accomplishment. It means I am making some incredible films. There are far more meaningful and important things to focus on. Life is hard enough without adding the extra burden of unrealistic expectation.

As I stood at the lectern of St Michael's Church, about to deliver the final words of my eulogy at the memorial service, I took a pause to stave off the uncontrollable sobbing that was about to engulf me. Repeatedly biting my lip until it bled seemed to help. I had managed to get to this point without crying but knew it was only seconds before the tears would flow. I barely managed to finish with the words of how I used to fear death, but this was something that no longer scared me. When my time inevitably comes, the thought of Rob's spirit welcoming me on the other side filled me with a relaxed feeling. Even the most minuscule drop of hope of that occurring was enough to calm my soul. With that I broke down in a flood of tears, the dam wall collapsed.

The power of his influence on my whole being is unmatched. He was a volcanic presence in my life. How blessed my parents were to have Rob as their son. How proud and eternally grateful my sister Sue and brothers Graham, Don, Ricky, and I are for being able to say … he was my brother.

EPILOGUE

It is 14 March 2022. 'How's the documentary going on Rob?' It was my dad on the other end of the phone. 'What do you mean documentary?' I said back to him. 'You know, the thing you are working on for Rob,' he said. 'Dad, I've told you it's not a documentary, it's a book,' I tried to say as politely as I could. 'A book,' he exclaimed. 'Do you know how to write a book?' 'Well, we will have to wait and see I guess,' I offered back. He continued this theme with, 'How do you do it? Are you writing with a pen or typing on to something?' 'Typing dad,' I said wearily, this conversation was getting old fast. 'Can you type?' he half yelled.' 'Yes, dad, I can type.'

As I eagerly tried to change the subject, I sensed he was really excited at the prospect of something coming out featuring Rob. This has been my motivation for writing this book. To give my family and relatives a reminder of who we were lucky enough to have in our lives.

I am under no illusions that each of them could write their own version of the Rob story. The same could go for his army of close friends. I'm certain I've missed many stories and events as there were simply too many to recall. But this is my version. It's purely an account of my relationship with my brother. I apologise to those who feel I have missed something. I will leave other people's personal accounts of life with Rob for them to tell.

I purposely omitted many very personal and private elements of Rob's life. The main one involves his wife Dusty and the children. This is not my place to speak on her behalf. As the years have passed, Dusty's contact with the Dickson family has slowly waned as she became more independent, which is fully understandable.

To get through the worst that life could throw at you, in the way she did, was simply incredible. She is a strong, brave woman. We love Dusty and always will. Our hearts are forever broken for her. But she has a new life now which is her own business, no one else's. We as a family wish nothing more than for her to be happy once again. She deserves nothing less.

Thank you to Galia and Alan Hardy. They have guided and supported me through the whole process. Thanks to Gillon McLachlan for his kind words in the foreword. I want to thank my family for assisting with stories and memories of Rob.

My wife Ness has been of monumental support to me throughout. Thank you, Ness. I love you.

To my three kids, Abby, Sasha and Luke, you mean everything to me. I hope this book will give you further insight into the person my brother Rob was. You should be very proud in the knowledge that Rob Dickson was your uncle. Love Dad. X